A QUESTION OF JOURNEY

by

D1706328

John Brandi

Light and Dust Books

1995

to Rosalinda
with Love
Always ♡

ISBN 0-87924-067-9

✣

Writings in this book have appeared in present or earlier forms in the following publications: *Blue Mesa Review, Cold Drill, Hawaii Pacific Review, Labrys, Luna Tack, Pax, River Styx, Kyoto Journal* and *Santa Fe News & Review.*

This book was made possible by the kind support of Mr. Stephen Finn *and* Sharon Philpott *from whose collection permission has been granted to reproduce the author's front cover collage:* "Kathmandu Canto."

✣

Printed on recycled paper with soy-based inks.

Published by:

Light & Dust Books
7112 27th Avenue
Kenosha Wisconsin 53143
Fax (414) 657-0324

Distributed by:

Small Press Distribution
1814 San Pablo Avenue
Berkeley, California 94702
(800) 869-7553

CONTENTS

PREAMBLE

In 1971, after spending two years in the Andes as a Peace Corps Volunteer and another couple of years between Mexico, Alaska and the California Sierra Nevadas as a war resistor, I moved to New Mexico. I had grown fond of arid uplifts, particularly those in which humans paid homage—through elaborate systems of ritual drama—to the unseen forces which turn the wheel of life. The Mexican sierras of the Huichol come to mind, as does the altiplano of Bolivia. With its crystal atmosphere, sparse horizon and elaborate indigenous ceremonies, New Mexico shared a similar identity. It would, over the next twenty years, become a well-suited base, a place where dream and reality converged, where one could live life without a marked division between either. It was locked within the United States yet was a country of its own: a weave of native languages, extraordinary ceremonials, crops of red chili and blue corn, violent sweet-scented desert thunderstorms, and quiet winter snow fringing earthen homes inseparable from the bizarre topography that backed them.

New Mexico nourished my spirit as a painter, writer, wanderer and homemaker. Native American traditions of song, dance and art in acknowledgement to the earth, air, water and sun that sustain all life reaffirmed my own belief systems. My children—daughter born in Guadalajara, son in a tiny Sangre-de-Cristo adobe house—grew up in the mountains of New Mexico, a rich outback which continues to feed them.

Many poems written during my first decade in the Southwest were collected in *That Back Road In*. I introduced them as "topographic or even typographic projections of the landscape" and viewed the book as a kind of emotional or psychic schematic of territory where "heart, mind, rock and mirage all overlap." I was curious to record everything: what people spoke; how they worked, sang and played; the look and feel of the land; each place and event that filled me with heightened tranquility and awe. The poems became a record of exploration: getting to know new territory, finding out who my neighbors were, investigating the hidden canyons of the self. In 1982 a collection of prose called *The Cowboy from Phantom Banks* was issued, later to be expanded and republished as *In the Desert We do not Count the Days*. Again, the focus was on the land and people of the high desert.

From 1979 on, my Southwest travels alternated with journeys into more remote deserts: those of Asia. Rajasthan, Ladakh, the uplands toward Tibet in the Himalayan rain shadow north of Mt. Annapurna. As in the Southwest, these places were filled with sacred sites, venerated waters and time-tested pilgrimage spots. There were also elaborate ceremonies: tribal, Hindu, Buddhist.

In New Mexico I used my home near Albuquerque as a place to be from and return to during hinterland explorations. In Asia I also used urban areas as bases from which to travel out, the difference being that those cities, particularly in India, were festering beehives of unintelligible languages, baffling customs, seething multitudes, deafening sounds, extreme poverty and an absence of privacy—experiences which juxtaposed themselves between backcountry ventures and became equally important to my writing.

Between 1980 and 1990 I exhibited paintings based on three sojourns to India, Nepal, Burma and Thailand. Simultaneously, I worked on journal notations which, via letters or in limited-edition xeroxes, were shared with friends. A few poems issued during this period in *Hymn for a Night Feast* and *That Crow That Visited Was Flying Backwards* gave a hint of the Asia experience. But the real work consisted of slowly compiling a book-length prose manuscript which eventually made way to publishers and was successively turned down.

One editor replied, "I wouldn't know what to call it, and not knowing what to call it how could I possibly market it?" Another swiveled on his expensive chair, eying the thickness of the spines of books he'd published (on a shelf above him under three clocks showing New York, London, and Tokyo times), and then looked down at my 150-page manuscript, judging its potential page number. After a short silence, he replied: "Not thick enough. The book must be more substantial. Give us more pages." Of course, I had spent years making it thin. Yet another publisher, whose travel books targeted the armchair traveler, refused the book on the grounds that "it raised too many questions our readers don't want raised, let alone answered."

Every time the manuscript came back I felt the usual depression of either not being understood or of having my work spit from a machine hopelessly concerned with trend, economics, a commonplace market and censorship. Then I came across a great excerpt from a talk given by Eduardo Galeano at an American Bookseller's Association conference:

> So many doubts about my own work. I ask myself: does literature have any role in this world where 5 year-olds are electronics engineers? And I try to answer: perhaps the life style of our times is not good for people or nature, but it is certainly good for the pharmaceutical industry. Why couldn't it also be good for the literary industry? It all

depends on the product you offer. Good books would have to be as tranquilizing as Valium, with a brilliant wrapper and a content that's "light." It should help people to think no risky thoughts and to feel no crazy feelings. It should help people to avoid dangerous dreams and above all avoid the temptation to live them. But this is exactly the literature I am unable to write or read. Doomed to impotence, I cannot write or read neutral words. And no matter how hard I try, I cannot stop believing that these times of resignation and falling prestige of human passion, when all unprofitable commitments are to be repented—these times are our challenge, not our destiny.

Concurrently, I discovered the poet Alain Bosquet's words, "essential writing raises wild notions and a challenge," and felt reinvigorated. In reading his poems I experienced the same disturbance that overcame me while writing about the world I had traveled in: that it was rapidly shrinking, tilting, clouding; that languages, the power to listen, observe and speak truthfully had nearly disappeared; that tradition, truths, remembrance, even a realistic concept of mortality, had vanished along with clean water, breathable air and a once-abundant population of beautiful, intelligent, necessary life species.

Such realizations made it clear that we need a psychic or physical transformation, and a challenge—unreasoned—to carry us beyond stale boundaries—mental and geographical—imposed by uninspired leaders and enforced by brutal regimes who disguise themselves in suits and ties and work predictable hours in "respectable" offices. One can stay at home and read about the world and realize these disturbances; or journey, experience the pathos, feel a small bit of joy in the lives of real people struggling with daily activities in real places, and know the tremendous odds presented by a heart-breaking world filled with nuclear arsenal, tree-toppled mountainsides, smuggled arms, slaughtered elephants, horrid atmosphere and a population that continues to explode.

A journey to Indonesia in 1993, focused on the island of Bali, brought me into a culture productively obsessed with art, music, theater, dance, insight, transformation; finding balance within the interplay of good and evil—and maintaining equilibrium within a complex weave of natural and supernatural forces. The Balinese idea of dance as a mix of song, ritual drama and theater performed (or "offered") outdoors, off stage, in village squares and earthen temple compounds, reminded me of Native American rituals in New Mexico.

"Being is difficult," Bosquet says. "Imagining is fruitful. The poem is tomorrow's truth. It offers the reader a secular prayer through which he can imagine new rapports between man and the universe, man and the void, man and himself." In agreement—except for the limiting word "man"—I offer this book, these journeys, as a means toward the transformation, the metamorphosis that Bosquet implies. Travel, step away from the familiar, touch, be touched. Leave home, let the unpredictability of the road shake your beliefs, find a new way back. Along the way become someone else. Perhaps this new he or she is the you that was there all the time, before you were defined or began to define that person who stares back from the mirror.

jb
New Mexico / 1994

"Even the man who is happy is touched with a longing
he does not recognize. It must be he is remembering
a place out of reach, shapes he had loved in a life before this, the print of
them still there inside him, waiting."

—Kalidasa

for Her

OLD DELHI, INDIA

The curbsides at twilight. The unending ritual of body against body adjusting itself for sleep. Moving bundles of rags. Coal-blackened, skeletal hands reaching to rearrange a makeshift cardboard pillow or wedge of packing foam. Bones protruding from torsos, eyes rolling lopsidedly in yellow sockets, ears deadened by booming factories, bell clang and piston wheeze. All evening and far into the night: no let up. Across the way, under smoke-darkened crisscross of steel beams, a sea of people writhes between spittle-stained columns in the railway station. Their tangled headscreams, obscene barks and shameless demands filter through sulfurous haze and mix with the tubercular coughs, the half-dream agonies and muffled conversations of the street sleepers whose bodies nest on hard cement.

The impossibility of India.

To say that the nation is poor is to bring to mind economic depression, starvation, the thirst for material goods. But its poverty begins with the multitude, the embedded system of caste and codes, the stifling effect of role upon role, death upon death, burning upon burning, birth and endless rebirth.

At dawn my room at the Hotel Shalay is filled with smoke. In the courtyard below, a whiskered broken-flagpole of a man fires up a clay hearth and overboils a soot-stained pot of milk tea. Two women carry head loads of thorny kindling through a portal. Another enters with a basket of fresh cow dung. The man does not offer them tea. He is first, then his brothers, now the male servants, lastly the children. Meanwhile, the women break the kindling into neat piles and begin mixing the cow dung with bits of charcoal and weeds. Rapidly, in the same manner that they slap out flat bread, they pat and shape balls of dung between their palms to form cakes for fuel used in cooking fires. Soon each perfectly-rounded paddy is pressed to the cement walls and window frames of the courtyard to dry. Within an hour there are dozens of these brown gleaming—geometrically arranged dung cakes scenting the air, covering the patio walls like children's mud pies, each bearing an auspicious handprint.

On a sagging cot next to me sleeps a Spanish man. He is tanned from adventures in the warm seas of Indonesia. Face down he snores in a soiled pillow, his forehead beaded with sweat. Fresh off the plane and disoriented by India, he found me among throngs of ambling shoppers and haggling merchants in the Chadni Chowk Bazaar. When he asked for directions to cheap lodging, I mentioned the Shalay. At which point he fumbled and moaned, trying to break free of the curious gawkers surrounding him, all tugging with suggestions of their own.

"I need out of here!"

The man pulled like a child at my sleeve. I quickly turned, spotted a rickshaw driver, hailed him, and agreed on a price for a ride to the Shalay. Within minutes, though, the ride turned to disaster. The rickshaw driver, hoping to convince the Spanish man of a different hotel and thus pick up a small commission from the manager, took a deliberately meandering route to the Shalay.

Deeper and deeper into the maddening crowd he pedaled, stopping first at the shop of a friend who sold hookahs; then to the brass vendor; now to a bristly-jawed man sitting cross-legged above off-register lithographs of Christ in a pipal grove with Buddha, both of them looking haggard and red eyed due to the bad printing. At each stop the rickshaw driver insisted we buy something. Opium. Phony marble antiquities. Chrome lingam. Ganja pipe. Plastic trident. Contraband shoes. Sun-damaged scarves printed with bliss-bestowing mantras. He was relentless, jabbering without stop, a baffling mix of Hindi and broken-textbook British, through a harmonica-row of missing teeth.

Each time his feet slowed on the pedals, sweat gathered on his back and soaked through his t-shirt. Bearing his thin weight again on the pedals, his ribs stood out, his mouth burped red spittle from an assortment of leaf-wrapped herbs rolled under his lip. Twice he was forced from his squeaking three-wheel bicycle rickshaw to repair the sagging chain that drove the rear wheels.

The Spanish man began to suffocate. He looked for a way out of the shoppers, the pushing mass of neon-lit skeletons, the rearing horses and bellowing bulls, the monkeys banging across tin roofs with scheming looks in their fiery eyes. The constant murmur of the crowd rose and fell in unstopping waves. Whips lashed the backs of draft horses. Movie soundtracks blared from crackling loudspeakers. Not for a second was there any pause. The Spanish man struggled as if in a web. He flapped his arms: a disoriented butterfly. Suddenly he stood up in the teetering carriage of the rickshaw, dangerously throwing the driver off balance on his little bicycle seat in front of us.

"Mucho mundo, mucho mundo!"

Spread eagle, the Spanish man leaped from the flimsy rickshaw, unable to withstand the thickening multitude, the desperate driver panting as he struggled to maneuver his flimsy contraption through it all. Everywhere poor animals with bleeding rumps lumbered beneath payloads of grain and potbellied high-class families. The Spanish man ran to a curb and shook like a broken bough. He sank into himself, refusing to be coaxed back into the rickshaw. In a daze, he pulled his arms around his shoulders and hung his head under the blinding fluorescent bars sagging over the silhouettes of tired vendors slumped over used bridal veils and spare sewing-machine parts. A group of tumorous beggars surrounded him. His shaggy head fell deeper between his palms as he coiled to the pavement, overwhelmed.

"Mucho mundo, mucho mundo!"

▨

Nothing has changed this morning. The Spanish man found his way back to the Shalay by foot. From the open window of our room I see the sidewalk sleepers still snoring on the sidewalk. The monkeys, the pundits, the tangled throngs go on as they did yesterday and yesteryear and decades before. The nervous India, the strangled India, is too tired to be anything but indifferent.

The crowded chessboard of India thick with flies and sweets. The raw-sewage India bright with silks, dreary with shut-eye homeless napping under dripping air conditioners in the white heat of day. The India filled with nameless ones who've come from nowhere, who're off to nowhere, whose legs do not end in feet, whose arms are too maimed to reach. A few manage to fold themselves into fetal balls and whine in silent

4

melodies to blot out the chaos. The rest are too hungry, too wrecked, too tired to reflect. There is no such thing as privacy, nothing of leisure time that the privileged know.

In the Old Delhi Station, a whistle screams.

The Spanish man wrinkles his brow then buries himself in his sheet. My eyes move away from the curbsides and courtyard below, and back again with a prayer in the face of civilization's dark madness. A tiny mantra for the *Mucho mundo, mucho mundo* of all these closely-packed bodies, thin and susceptible, jammed together by colonizers, bred in the city's huge cage for no other reason than to work and to suffer, to be cast into molds, to pray and be preyed upon.

▓

TAJ MAHAL, ENIGMA AND REALITY

"Sahib, look!"

The conductor on the Rajdhani Mail Express, a leathery-skinned man with huge eyebrows and a bright smile, taps me on the shoulder, pointing with his black glove out the window. Across the early-morning landscape, a few kilometers off, is the Taj, a marble jewel box on a pink sandstone base floating above a graceful brush stroke of lavender mist rising over flooded fields and waving sugarcane.

"A supreme sight, Sahib!"

The train chuffs on, lacing the open window with a fiery blizzard of cinders. Crows fly into the calligraphed shadow of engine smoke. Here and there, between the waving sugarcane, tattered children laugh, poke their heads, mimic the puffing train and extend their hands toward the passengers, or rub their stomachs and extend begging arms. These are human scarecrows, kids paid the equivalent of a few cents a day to chase ravens from rice paddies with slingshots and pebble-filled cans.

The train slows for a curve, then grudgingly regains momentum. As we near Agra city, the Taj grows in proportion, yet by some architectural mystery it gains neither weight nor solidity. Its domes and minarets seem fashioned from a transparent material that both absorbs light and ricochets it back into the beholder's eye. The atmosphere is mottled with blues, greys, shimmering violets—a Monet painting. The paradox of its beauty lies in the fact that its painterly splendor is created through subtle layering of pollution from thousands of brushwood hearth fires, the dust of goat and cow herds, the ugly coal haze and acidic fumes from Agra's industry.

Another paradox: the more momentum the train gains, the more I seem to be standing still within its carriage. It is the Taj that moves, a rotating music box suspended just slightly above a foreground of chartreuse and mirrored blue. Its measurements are exact. Its towers align perfectly. The sheer marble walls, inlaid with hundreds of thousands of precious stones, reflect the rising sun like a master-cut diamond. If this could be my only glimpse of the Taj it would suffice for a lifetime.

※

The locomotive slows. Agra is within range. The Taj disappears from view, replaced by a tangle of dusty trees, rotting shanties, clanging rickshaws, a fly-dotted labyrinth of sweet shops and tea stalls whose gloomy interiors hide behind bamboo scaffolding webbed with electric wire. The whistle screams. A pathetic stationmaster runs after his hat in churning dust and grind of braking wheels. In a vaporous frenzy of steam and grease, without any plan of direction or thought of courtesy, the passengers—so amiable during the journey—deboard. Farmers shove, invalids fall, upper caste swing parasols, children slither between crotches and fat bellies. A hundred red-turbaned porters grab for boxes, bulging suitcases, mattresses and overstuffed baskets. The station platform is rancid with urine, crushed mangos, red spittle, puddled debris of splintered sugarcane and tea leaves.

I hail a horse-drawn tonga away from the oppressive crowd and consumptive beggars, past a 16th-century sandstone fort begun by the

Mogul ruler Akbar, then along the Jumna River's graceful curve, where finches go about nest building—stealing human hair from public spigots where Hindu women bathe and a great banging of metal cookware chimes through the air. Here, the famous dome of the Taj finally reappears. A dome that replicates the bulbous haystacks dotting hand-sickled fields across the river. A dome said to have its origins in bell-shaped tents of Tartars, the fat snow-crests of the Himalayas, the mosques of Persia, the lotus bud, or symbolic milk-swollen breasts of mothers nursing their young.

At the arched entrance through the south wall of the Taj is a sneezing skeleton of a man inside a caged hole who collects money for the Seventh Wonder of the World. He hands me a dirty ticket, walks out of the cage to collect it from me, then tears it neatly in half to make it official. I walk through a dark and massive sandstone gateway and—yes—there before me is a Wonder, indeed.

I stroll a few paces. A bristly-chinned groundskeeper has eyed me from over his broom and is quickly by my side, speaking without hesitation. "You are impressed? Is it not awful to have come from so far and *not* be impressed!" He is a jovial old timer from Mathura, the legendary birthplace of the god Krishna. For fifteen years he has been employed by the Government of India Tourist Office. His sole duty: to sweep pigeon droppings from two-thousand square feet of walkway surrounding the pools of the Taj, a task which he seems content to perform—with the ingenious help of a dead crow which he has strung from an acacia tree overhanging the main walkway.

"The crow scares away the pigeons. That way I do not have so many droppings to sweep. I have more time to talk to people like you. I tell

9

everybody the same thing. Visit the Taj many times. Early day. Sunset. When the moon is large. Each time you visit bring less of yourself. Less of what you have been told about the Taj. Then you will finally begin to see it as it is, to find personal meaning."

The groundskeeper points to a calligraphed verse from the Qu'ran inscribed in jet on the southern facade of the great archway through which I've strolled. Here, the stonemasons and calligraphers labored jointly to make the size of the script seem uniform to the eye, even though it recedes further from the eye as it proceeds up the arch.

"In reality we have an illusion. The size of the letters appears identical. But it is not. The letters grow in dimension near the top of the arch. From where we stand the size of the script, no matter where you look, equalizes itself within the eye. Everywhere you walk—in the gardens, in the chambers of the tomb, around the minarets—you will find this attention to illusion."

▨

High noon. I have still not approached the monument proper. The groundskeeper has returned to his task of chipping away the hardened pigeon droppings with a putty knife. I have lingered in the sensual formality of the Persian gardens that eventually open through a hedged labyrinth into the main pathway leading up to the evanescent womb of the mausoleum. Amusing—my attempt to relax, focus, bring "meaning" to this event, all the while impeded by the mind's tricks.

First it goes about convincing me of the "importance" of being here. Then it tries telling me I might not really be really here. Next, the tantalizing "facts" of history, things of consequence that are supposed to magnify my appreciation of the edifice. How emperor Shah Jahan planned the Taj as a memorial to his young wife, Mumtaz Mahal, the Beloved of the Palace who died bearing his fourteenth child as he was off waging battle. How he wept afterwards, his hair turning white within days of her passing. How he summoned architects, stonecutters, astronomers, mosaicists and silversmiths from Persia, Arabia, Afghanistan, the Mediterranean and all of India to make his personal vision—a tomb for the Chosen One—a public reality. How he commissioned 20,000 laborers for two decades to complete his vision. How, as legend has it, he severed the hands of his architects and blinded them to prevent them from ever replicating the Taj.

And, finally, how he was imprisoned by his own son who didn't wish to see his madman of a father squander any more of his inheritance money on more public monuments. In the Red Fort, a short distance away from his beloved wife's mausoleum, Shah Jahan died, locked away from the world, supposedly from an overdose of aphrodisiacs while attempting to seduce two female servants. In the Jasmine Tower of his ruling quarters, the great Mogul king expired on a cot near a tiny window from which the marble dome over Mumtaz's cenotaph was reflected by means of a tiny mirror angled exactly into the retinas of his dying eyes.

"Yes, splendid?"

The Chaplinesque groundskeeper twinkled his eye and shook his head puppet-like side to side as he ladled pigeon droppings into his battered wheelbarrow.

Now the mind switched from history and legend and began with symbolism, filling me with the secret meaning of the gardens where I lingered. Quite possibly their roses and weeping trees corresponded with Eden. Paradise on earth. Not a heaven saved for afterlife, but a metaphysical oasis. A metaphor for the inner womb of spiritual rebirth. A walled refuge of transition between the outer world of sensual pleasure and the psychic garden of ephemeral quests.

Suddenly the daze of shifting impressions pops. I look up and find myself surrounded by itinerant masseurs with boxes of incense, oils, towels. One squeezes my ears, another rubs my spine, bends my arms backwards, oils my toes and begins to pull them forward asking if I have something to sell. Watch? Levis? Calculator? An official hurries them off, but in turn pesters me with the usual Indian repertoire: Where from? What do? Married? Children? Where staying? Change money? How long in India? What size shoe?

※

Late afternoon. Heatwaves from smooth marble. Breezeless silver sky. Egrets on cows' backs in the smoking fields across the shallow Jumna. I remove my shoes, pass through a tunnel, up a stairway and onto the pink sandstone platform from which rises the Taj. Pilgrims. Tourists. Tour groups. Here, they all converge, ooh and awe, flash their bulbs, adjust lenses, change film cartridges, read tour books and sip overpriced, oversweetened crimson sodas under the broiling sun. In khaki pants and socks, white turban and flowing white shirt, a tall Sikh gestures emphatically. As he speaks, his handle-bar mustache moves up and down in front of a tour group—everyone madly fanning themselves with silk scarves and straw hats.

"Now we stand above River Jum-naa. Best known river in India except for Gan-gaa. Just north of here are many favorite scenes of visit. Jumna banks are where Lord Krishna, eighth avatar of Hindu god Vishnu, played with his favorite cowgirls. Just across from us in those fields, other side of Jum-naa, is where Shah Jahan wished to build his own tomb, exact replica of the Taj. Except it was to be black. Made of pure jet. With pure silver bridge spanning the river, connecting it with his wife's tomb. Try to imagine. Take a moment of silence . . ."

In the stifling heat the tour group becomes quickly restless. A few saunter back to the soda stand at the main entrance. Others swat flies and search for relief, lifting one, then the other foot from the sizzling stone. In the shadow of a minaret I take refuge, my back to the Taj until almost sunset. From here the view over the Jumna arcs across to the fields where the setting sun sinks like a fat persimmon into Agra's pollution. The Jumna's placid waters are broken only by a small raft's eddy, quietly being paddled across river exactly where Shah Jahan's symbolic bridge would have been constructed. A man and a woman sit facing one another in the raft, hyacinth leaves and melons piled around them. A welcome breeze picks up, and with it come odors of wet fields and dung, plaintive singing from women in blazing silks carrying twigs in their arms and babies in baskets on their heads.

My eyes lift and turn back to the Taj. The tourists are gone. A playful wind licks the walkways. Across the Jumna flow the women's voices, a cart wheel creaking, the bellow of oxen. I place my hands, my cheeks, my tongue, my body against the smooth marble edifice, walking around it like a cat. Every mother-of-pearl inlay, each carnelian rose, every symmetrical representation of fruit (life) or cypress branch (death) becomes a floating galaxy of jade, agate, coral and lapiz in the snowy

13

brilliance of surrounding marble. Circumambulating the monument, lingering against its facades, my body feels an unexpected reconciliation with nature, with death and stone and sunlight.

This is not an opaque architecture, but a translucent embodiment of roots, leaves, whirling petals. A great white trunk whose presence, in the luxuriant garden which surrounds, is sonorous, carnal; a simultaneous evocation of heat and snow; the very essence of the effects of light and ice one encounters in the Himalayas where, ironically, I once stood spellbound, muttering: "after *this* , why visit any man-made temple?"

Slowly, as the groundskeeper predicted, the Taj becomes personal. Its pearly, albescent walls cause me to remember that forty years ago my own father stood here, marveling at this same sight. He kept a diary, took photos and returned to America bearing souvenirs from Agra which he presented to me as a baby: a slender brass vase engraved with spiraling vines; a bronze bell cast in the shape of the Taj Mahal's dome; a little hand-carved alabaster box whose lid was inlaid with a mother-of-pearl replica of the Taj. All three objects, fashioned by India's artists from the earth's minerals, were carried across the Pacific and unwrapped in the rich sunlight beneath our backyard lemon tree. They exuded a peculiar presence when I pressed them to my mouth. The strong odor of the metals, the melodious vibration of the bell's song, the alabaster's warmth against my cheeks: here were the symbols and realities of an exotic land, the seeds of my present journey.

Little did I know, still crawling on hands and knees, unable to sense the greater proportions of the world, that these "toys" were a calling—unintended by my father—toward the urge to wander, to escape that walled garden of childhood where normalcy ruled and protective figures directed.

Somewhere within the grounds of the Taj a bell rings . . .

The echo converses with itself, then oscillates through the cooling mauve of dusk into my ears. I remember a famous Persian couplet inscribed in gold by Shah Jahan in his Hall of Private Audience in the Red Fort at New Delhi:

> *"If there be a paradise on earth*
> *then this is it, yes this is it, this is it."*

※

The body becomes still in the Taj Mahal's presence. Up close or from afar, the mind loses itself in architecture at once real, at once ephemeral. Architecture constructed to immortalize the flesh, to release the spirit of a loved one back into the world of mortals, and to allow mortals themselves to pass through perforated screens of light to enter a world beyond. Each tower, every room, each crevice, hallway, tunnel and portico is a secret recess of the unconscious. Precious lacework of pearl cornices, fiery bursts of sacred verse, arches and galleries gloaming with fireweed and anemone. Fanciful birds singing from quarried stone fashioned into spandrels and domes. A chrysolite lotus with an all-seeing eye at center. These engulf one's presence, cause the Taj to lift, float and spin from a distance, or—up close—open the body with light, lead the psyche into shadowy gauze of memory.

The enigma of the Taj is its reality. A reality which both lures and repels, gives rise to myth, marks historical as well as allegorical time, all the while revealing Shah Jahan's passionate yet decadent fervor. The splendor of its whiteness paradoxically opens a door to our nocturnal selves. Within its chambers we leap from sunlight to shadow, human to sacred realms. The marble's softness, the dazzle of *pietra dura,* the sun's fragmenting interplay upon the monument's contours and perforations evokes dream, awakens lost moments, attempts to define the absolute.

One traveler called Mumtaz Mahal's tomb "solidified music." A tour guide said "love and death united." From the window of the Rajdhani Mail Train the Taj is pure apparition. Something magical constructing itself before your eyes while the rails speed you along and sparks shower your vision. Rising from a misty garden, from imagination's green fields, from India's auspicious squalor, the Taj spins into an opalescent dervish dancing in a natural paradise where imagination and reality are void of boundaries; a garden where one man's inspiration manifests itself in a public hymn: an ethereal cantata whose lyrical brilliance symbolizes life after death, a spiritual beginning.

Up close, in the last moments of dusk, I stand back, body warmed by the still-radiating stone, voice softly uttering the last line of the Persian couplet inscribed by Emperor Shah Jahan in his Hall of Visitation:

"Yes this is it, this is it."

❈

WOMEN OF THE WEST, MEN OF THE EAST

"P.V.L.P. Babu" sat directly across from me, a screw salesman from Delhi on his way to Madras. It was a second-class train, agonizingly tardy with innumerable stops, one of them at three in the morning in a steamy town just north of the River Krishna. There was a bridge out up ahead. Railroad workers hired to repair the bridge had accidentally set its timbers aflame while lighting a bonfire to keep warm. So the story went.

Instantly, the sleepy hamlet north of the River Krishna sprung to life. Lights were lit. Townsfolk appeared in balconies and doorways like figurines mechanically animated in a Black Forest cuckoo clock. Vendors wheeled out their carts. Ancient Victrolas were cranked full. The townsfolk seemed quite prepared for this unscheduled delay. P.V.L.P. Babu winked and said, "It happens often."

Next morning, just north of Madras, there was another delay. A *bidi* flicked from the coach in front of ours had lodged in the rubber boot between the carriages and was dangerously smoldering. Smoke permeated the air. Passengers were nervous. As the fumes increased people packed the aisle, making ready for the exits. P.V.L.P. Babu eyed me reassuringly, reached for an emergency chain dangling above the barred window, and pulled. The rusty chain snapped from the ceiling and the screw salesman tossed the handle out the window in disgust.

I looked around. A group of men were gathered in the aisle beside my seat, jabbering as they moved in, pointing at the red trousers I'd purchased in Dharmsala. "They want you to remove your pants," Babu explained. "They want to use them to wave down the engineer and stop the train."

The men moved closer, holding up a towel behind which I was supposed to undress. "How can they do this?" I stammered.

"An emergency . . . " Babu frowned.

At that moment, as if born from the all-seing eye of Avalokiteshvara, a Tibetan peddler strapped with a wooden tray of bright acrylic sweaters walked into the coach, oblivious to what was happening. Immediately the jabbering men yanked a blaze-orange sweater from the vendor and waved it out the window as the train rounded a bend. The engineer halted and the fire was extinguished with handfuls of sand.

When the journey resumed, P.V.L.P. proudly commended the efficiency with which his countrymen handled the danger. Then he sat upright, hands folded on top of his black briefcase, and eyed me squarely with that particularly uncanny look of an Indian man about to explore the foreigner's psyche.

"We will now talk of women," P.V.L.P. Babu explained.

Here it comes, I thought. And indeed it did. He wanted to know all about Western women. Why they traveled alone. Why they were not married. Why they wore blouses which bared their backs. And finally, what "proper formula" could a man like him employ to get to know a Western woman? When I smiled and advised him that I had no formula—just do what comes natural, let chemistry govern—he became sullen.

"You speak figuratively," he chided.

It was impossible for this middle-aged screw salesman, raised in a world of codified relationships and arranged marriages, to envision such spontaneity. He opened his briefcase. Screws. Comic books. A clean pair of boxer shorts. And a fingermarked envelope which he placed in my lap.

"Please, see. In India we do it this way."

The envelope contained P.V.L.P.'s collection of want ads clipped from the Northern Patrika newspaper.

> Wanted: Hindu groom or any Brahmin boy for two homely girls 24 & 21. Smart appearing, immediate marriage.

> Please: healthy tall wheat-complected girl match for handsome bachelor. Respectable family, affluent. Sub caste and local employment no bar. Slim figure. No dowry.

> Suitable bride: for M.M.B.B.S. Nationalized-bank employed young man. Must be fair.

He folded the ads into tiny squares, stuffed them nervously back into the soiled envelope, and bent close to me. He whispered, then, a slithering whisper which smelled of the herbs he was chewing.

21

"I want to talk of a bad experience. It was when I leased a tea shop in the Saharanpur train station. A modest shop—posters of movie stars, scenes of Kashmir, clean cups, coffee from the south, tea from Assam. And quite often frequented by foreigners who I helped with tickets and directions between trains. Once, a pretty brunette sat down, alone. I could not take my eyes from her. I served her light black tea, the way Western people like. I sat with her and tried to talk.

"When I asked her why she was in India she said 'to know the culture.' And I thought, ah this is my entry. I asked her to come home for dinner. I worked hard to convince her. Finally she said yes. I closed the shop early and off we rode on my scooter. At home she was surprised that I had no wife, no family. She did not seem to enjoy being alone with me. I poured her an imported rum to settle her fears, but she refused it. My plan for relaxing her into further conversation did not seem to be working. When she got up to use the water closet I attempted to add rum to her Coca Cola. But she caught me. She became emotional and I thought, now is a good time to kiss her. I started up her arm, trying to calm her. I had rehearsed this technique many times on my own arm. But she was becoming hysterical, demanding that I take her back to the station. I had had a lot to drink. I could not start my scooter and we had to walk the five kilometers to the station. She missed her train. I pleaded for her to stay at my place. 'Never!' she screamed at me. And hurried off to look for a hotel. That was the end of the evening. And I thought, why was I punished like that? Why sleeping alone when just hours before I almost had her. Almost!"

The whistle blew. The screw salesman shrugged his shoulders; his face became blank. "Clearly I missed a great opportunity. What do you say?" But the train was already at the Madras station, passengers were

22

scrambling for the exits. In the madness P.V.L.P. Babu and I parted without formality.

❈

At Kalpana's Cafe in downtown Madras, I wondered whether to drink the ice water in the stainless steel tumbler before me, aware that across the aisle a conservatively-bearded man with horn-rim glasses and a well-pressed sport shirt was observing my every move.

"Speak your name to the water. Speak it directly. The water shall become pure."

The man smiled and waited. His friend—tall and slender, wearing a red turban, white shirt and shark-skin trousers—also smiled. Within minutes the two of them joined me and clapped their hands for tea and a saucer of sweets. They introduced themselves as Mohinder and Pommi—Hindu and Sikh. Mohinder was very forward. He held up my tumbler, stared upward, and proceeded into a long monologue about the vibratory power of the word: "With right intent and pronunciation, each syllable of one's own name can rearrange the molecular structure of the elements, purify them, transform them."

His gestures were exaggerated. His booming voice filled the cafe. Was he out to test my beliefs or setting me up for something a tourist might like to hear from an Indian? Both. As we conversed, Mohinder revealed himself as a professional actor, an experienced playwright, part of the lively underground of Madras. His eyes scanned the high, embossed tin ceiling of Kalpana's, the samovars on the shelves, the exotic trees and parading elephants painted on the walls.

He fixed his gaze on me and laughed a high whistle through his thin mouth. "I am giving you sadhu talk. The kind foreigners expect in this 'mystical' country of mine. It is part of a drama I am working on. A play that has to do with perception and deception. By the end of the final act the audience will have been assured that we are always being fooled by illusion and assumptions. That we are never closer to reality than what myth chooses to reveal."

Pommi was reserved compared to Mohinder. He did not gesture wildly, but listened intently even though his eyes were forever scanning Kalpana's array of customers. At length a strawberry-blond woman passed our booth, wearing a sari and a nose ring, bangles jingling on both wrists.

"Not Indian, " Pommi analyzed.
"Just a woman of the West trying on the clothes of India."

The young lady washed her hands at a basin at the rear of the cafe, took a nearby booth, ordered vegetarian and ate a mound of rice with the proper hand. Pommi watched her carefully, then turned to me, using the occasion to expound on his favorite subject: women.

From his imported Velcro wallet he unfolded a plastic accordion filled with photos of European women: the sandy-headed Swede he escorted through the mathematical regularity of a Kashmiri rose garden; the buxom, wide-eyed Belgian with whom he toured Khajuraho's erotic temples; the Modigliani-faced girl he made love to underwater at Kovalam; the French hippie dressed in translucent silk—the one he rescued from the monkeys in Maharashtra.

Most of his hard-earned paychecks were devoted to the seduction of these "promiscuous" foreigners. When his wallet was exhausted and his body drained from every conceivable position in the *Kama Sutra*, he returned to Madras, slept for days and resumed work as an installations man at his father's air-conditioning factory.

"I love Western women," he boasted quietly. "But they are not my final destiny. I will marry the bride of my family's choice. That will be in three more years. When I reach age thirty. Western women are good experience. But my bride is waiting, and she will be virgin. Indian. Of my own Sikh community, selected by my parents. She is my destiny. After our marriage it will be only her. I know who she is but I have not spoken to her. It is not yet time."

Pommi, unlike P.V.L.P. Babu, was comfortable with western women, admittedly using them as a kind of foreplay to the preselected Indian bride waiting at the top of his stairway. Yet both men had in common an adherence to tradition, an inability to cut through the tangles of religious and familial expectations which they were not supposed to question.

"I deal with it all on stage," Mohinder said, cleaning his glasses with his shirt tail. "Easterners and Westerners are in this together." He pointed to the reversed letters on the inside of the cafe's front window. "You know what Kalpana means? It means 'mind' . . 'imagination.' What we make the world into. Whoever we are, whatever we wear, no matter the color of our eyes or skin, we all partake in the same emotions. We are wrapped differently, that's all. Mind makes the wrapping, society ties the bow. My play will unwrap the package."

Mohinder scraped a living through part-time employment at his uncle's candle factory. He hooked up with tourists, found them cheap airline tickets, took his cut. Pommi, on the other hand, succumbed to tourists. By night's end, his daytime earnings would be drained, his guests' bellies full. He claimed to be making the best of the situation until his chosen one was ceremoniously handed over.

And women of the West, did not they too desire Pommi for experience? To see him with his turban removed, waist-length hair unknotted falling over his sleek, dark body? His mysterious silence broken, his handsome face turned upon them with passion?

Mohinder did not have the gentle attitude of Pommi, his charm or mystique. He was intense, overbearing, sinking quickly into dark introspection, rising unexpectedly with sudden exclamations tilting the deck of Kalpana's until the prow was weighted into a turbulent ocean, food spilling off tables, waiters waiting to catch the plates as Mohinder feigned a tablecloth stunt. Then up he stood, straightening into an icon—hands folded, steamy eyes red-rimmed behind his glasses, looking straight into India's soul, his mouth quivering:

"Prisoners! We are prisoners of our land! Prisoners of karma! Prisoners of the gods of tradition, and of this new god called 'fad' which demands we be up with the times. Why? Let us purify. Simplify. Untie our tongues. Wake to the lessons of experience. Let us unbalance, so we can rebalance! Who can go back to British India, Aryan India, Dravidian India? Who can go forward, either, into satellite India, nuclear India, casteless India? We are roped like the American beef cow in a grade-B movie. We are in the dust and we cannot move!"

He looked at me with hands on hips as if to draw a pistol. His glasses slipped down his nose. He hung his arms limply in the air like Christ on his cross, looking from side to side with wheezing gasps. All was in vortex, out of control. No lifeboat appeared, no one heard, and here he was, Mohinder the Crucified, voice blubbering as if sinking for the third time.

"Look at Pommi. If he were to fall in love—as you Westerners put it—with a beautiful girl from France or America, he would lose India forever. He would marry a foreigner and become a social outcast, a tourist in his own country. Better to be an untouchable! An untouchable still has caste. But a tourist is nothing. Nothing! You understand? A tourist has no family.

"And this notion of freedom. Who is free? The West's freedom leads to madness, too many alternatives. Men act like women. Women act like men. Families do not live together. People have no ritual or stories or history to call their own. And here in India? No freedom either. Too much history, too many rituals. Men and women repressed by heritage, not strengthened by it.

"In your country what do you do? Fall in love, marry, move away, look forward to divorce? In India what do we do? Marry, then meet and face the bigotry of in-laws? Individuals do not decide on marriage. I make no decision, Pommi makes none. Everybody lives at home, and home is a very large tree. Too strong to be cut down."

Mohinder was the fanatic Hindu, shifting positions as he talked, not always comfortable in the new territory into which his monologues probed. He didn't get along with Muslims and often spoke sorely of any reality outside India. But he was a dedicated artist, and for all his religious props and preaching, it was Mohinder who would—over the next couple

27

of weeks—snap alive the city's underworld for me. He loved the rebel poets Kabir and Chandidas. He knew the various alleys where mask makers, actors, costume designers, ventriloquists and balladeers went about their professions; where gypsies gathered with guitars and tarot cards; where the opium and ganja were traded.

Pommi balanced Mohinder's fiery outbursts with his even temper and good nature. He could obtain visa extensions, write medical excuses for visitors wishing to overstay their air travel returns. He had a special talent for dealing with the bureaucracy on a decent, rational level. If the train to Bhubaneswar or Darjeeling was full and you needed immediate booking, Pommi miraculously had the tickets. If you were in a quandary over a quick, safe black-market money exchange, fear not—Pommi tied the strings.

Mohinder and Pommi were the keys to an entire network of people unavailable to the casual visitor. There was a Dhaka minstrel who had spent a year in solitude, living on insects, composing songs to the cry of the Indian cuckoo whose notes, he claimed, equaled the perfect fifth of the Indian octave. There was Usha Gupta who performed modern dance at Tiruchirappalli, who pointed to her shoulder blades claiming they were evidence of where wings had been. There was Tulsi Baba, a shiny broad-faced man who earned a living behind stage screens producing sound effects from a pair of rubbery lips: a howler monkey, a ricocheting bullet, two lovers climaxing behind banging shutters, a spinning propeller, the crackle of locusts attacking a wheat field, the thud of a suicide victim plummeting from a skyscraper. No obstacle impossible for Mr. Baba.

Once, in Kalpana's, Mohinder examined a marble-topped table where a friend once stood on his head and spun. "A rather crazy actor who played

Hanuman in the Ramayana performances in the outdoor theater at Madurai's Sri Meenakshi temple. Devi Lal. He had the eyes of a dragonfly, the body of a bear, wore copper amulets around his arms and legs, devoured Vodka and loved to whirl. The waiters would bring that marble table into the center of the floor and Devi Lal would stand on his head, tuck in his arms to cut the air drag, and spin for a whole evening to the accompaniment of a clarinet trio. Six weeks later he would be walking around with a big, black scab on his head. Then we would all greet him as Kali Lal and he would look at us with crossed eyes, stick out his tongue and say, 'Time for me to see my head doctor.'"

No point in questioning Mohinder's stories. He would only put on a serious face, roll his eyeballs, feign a scholarly pompousness and assume a heavy accent—a smile breaking from one corner of his mouth: "Indeed, a very tenuous world in which we of India dwell, one where fusions of myth and history outrage the mind. As we write, words invent us. The moment an event is told it becomes real. In the end it is not a question of belief or disbelief, but whether a story works for you or not."

Last time I saw these men of the East, they were side by side in Kalpana's Cafe. Mohinder was mocking Indian bureaucracy, swirling one arm over his head like a ceiling fan, imitating a stack of fluttering papers on the table with his other, making sputtering noises from his puckered mouth. Pommi, he was sitting straight up, his elegant red turban worn proudly like a tribal headdress, his dark, manicured hands folded a hair's breadth from another pair of hands: those of the sunburnt woman across from him, a woman with short, golden hair and an intrigued smile on her face—a woman of the West.

✻

THE FERVOR OF THE CHILDREN AT JAISALMER

Dawn . . .

A soft, amber glow over India's Thar Desert. The ancient city of Jaisalmer sits on a dry mesa, half deserted, its stone buildings and 12th-century Jain temples barely distinguishable from their rocky bluff. Everything is stone: alabaster, sandstone, limestone. The spired temples and dusty rococo mansions gleam like ingots in the rising sun. The setting calls to mind Arizona's Hopi villages lifted into the sky on their golden mesas. Stone speaking to stone. Weightless solidity edged toward heaven. Spires, ladders, stairways joining the human spirit with the ethereal realm of the gods. Below, fanning out toward every point of the compas, a dry and silent sea undulates with rosy sand cresting and falling in gentle waves, tinting cloud bottoms pink as they roll in with the monsoon.

My room is in a partly-restored 17th-century *haveli*, mostly vacant, whose stairwells haven't seen a broom in years, whose storehouse doors have giant keyholes exuding musty odors of guano, incense, stale perfume and folded cloth that never made it to market. The landlord tells me the haveli is just another sprawling mansion meeting its decay as more and more residents abandon Jaisalmer for modern life in Jodhpur, Delhi or Bombay. Below the walled city, at the bottom of the mesa, a new town has sprung up hosting a military base and tourist bungalows. "A more convenient life," the landlord says. "Flat, no steep hills to climb. Close to the railway. And cleaner. There's a water system. No cisterns. Some of the tourist bungalows even have flush toilets. There's a video palace too."

He recalls stories told by his grandfather when Jaisalmer was a splendid town—no electricity, no rail connections. An oasis on the camel route between India and Persia. Rich, until Bombay and Calcutta became major trade channels and the British created partition. "After the split, tension increased. Wars with Pakistan interrupted trade. Commerce shut down. The military arrived. Opium, rare silk, precious oils, livestock, food from river valleys east of here—all of it ceased. Now it's aluminum pans, Seiko watches, automatic rifles. And, pardon me friend—you want some good Afghan ganja?"

❋

The streetside window in my third-story room is screened with filigreed alabaster. The airy design imitates a woman's veil. Stand behind it and you can see out, but who is seen can't look in. It was, and still is, customary for Jaisalmer's ladies to hide behind silk and stone in the shadows of their inner selves and watch the world go by. In the opposite wall there is a similar window that funnels a cool draft between its fretted stone. I peer through it far down into the haveli's kitchen courtyard. There, three women sit around a clay hearth cooking lentils in a large clay pot.

One smokes a water pipe. Another slaps chapatis. The third suckles her newborn while feeding sticks to the fire. Their gossip echoes with complaints and on rare occasion, laughter. The view down has a mineral clarity about it. The women, dressed in Rajasthani vermilions and canary yellows, wearing glass bangles and gold earrings, shimmer like agates at the bottom of a pool.

The haveli is centuries old, but it conveys not so much the passing of time as it does the passing of human lives through time. A bygone splendor is implied. The frescoes on my room's upper walls, once bright with elaborate color, have faded and chipped, revealing here and there part of a strutting peacock; a coiling vine; Krishna's arm tugging at Radha's sari; a dancer's foot, but no leg; a blue flute, but no pair of lips to play it; the penetrating eyes of a deva, but no face. As if smudged from the vapors of a hookah pipe in repeated use, the lower walls are stained a deep liquor color. Maybe this was the favorite room of a rich merchant. One where he enjoyed his opium, meditating on the erotic murals above his head (one shows a maiden holding a mirror to her secret parts) while he held a mirror to the beauties of his own love.

"Radha and Krishna," the landlord tells me, "are painted in bedrooms like this, to help newlyweds meditate on the pleasures of physical union. But there is cause for greater reflection. It is said that when Vishnu was alone in heaven he longed for pleasure. Radha and Krishna were beamed from his body and from their union came Brahma, who we believe is nature itself, the pure vibration of Krishna and Radha's lovemaking."

※

Perched on the mansion's flat roof, I scan the landscape. With no city below, there would be little scale to the immense desert beyond. Human presence, the pathos of its tumbling stone creations, the Babel-like reach of the hand toward God: all are lost to the desert's blinding immensity. As night falls, saffron thunderheads crackle and boom. Each blast of lightning shakes the old stone stairways and verandahs, puts new cracks in the domes and alcoves. The whole episode seems orchestrated by a smiling Force whose sole intent is to deflate the egos of the human architects that gave splendor to Jaisalmer.

When all is soaked and the storm marches off with blazing wings, an evening drama unfolds on the rooftop below my perch. A family is in process of unrolling its bedding. An old man sets up a flimsy charpoy made of wooden legs and webbed string, watches it collapse, sets it up again. A grandmother tries to quiet a pack of frolicking children who aren't much interested in sleep, but more intent on chasing their shadows in the hissing light of a kerosene lamp. Dogs yelp and fight and finally curl up, each in their proclaimed doorway. The parrots shriek to be covered, the cats scratch and whine for a few sad crumbs of moldy chapati. The lightning's beyond the rim now. Blue castles sleep under a brocade of gold pollen.

As I look I write. As I write I dream.

The mind is a magic carpet from an Arabian tale scrolling outward to the world's other side: to the Mojave Desert where I first gained appreciation of endless, unoccupied space; to the high grasslands of New Mexico where Navajos enact healing ceremonies with sweats, songs and sand paintings; to northern Arizona where Hopi dancers choreograph amazing ritual dramas, imploring nature to bring rain; to Mexico's deserts where the Yaquis transform themselves into deer to the beat of a water drum or the Huicholes walk their long walk into the mythical land of Wirikuta, chewing hallucinogens. In all of these places I am brought closer to the idea of true home—one where dream and reality merge and the beholder not only appreciates supreme Mystery, but participates in it.

░

Days in Jaisalmer pass.

I walk into the desert, feel its presence, return before the afternoon heat descends and nap. In sleep an incident from the morning reappears: a mad girl rests in the sand under an acacia tree. A lone flute player accompanies her, playing a sweet melody as he oversees his goats. In a trance, the girl sits up and speaks to herself, points to the goats and falls back to the sand, a pearly color around her body, a flowering branch shadowing her face. At the base of the tree a royal peacock cries, at which the girl again rises, mutters something and softly collapses.

"Was she mad or am I just thinking that?" I asked the landlord upon my return. "Not mad," he mused. "It is just that she had work to do—in dreams." Such as it is, this Indian land. Incidents one might dig for in the imagination, they are readily accessible in reality.

But what is this?

I hear the girl's voice again, the sound of the flute too. Up from my nap, standing at the streetside window, I look down to find both goatherd and girl there with a scruffy group of children getting ready for a street performance in a makeshift theater. I laugh at my former assumption. The girl was not mad, she was merely practicing her lines. And the goatherd, probably revising his flute song while tending his family's flock. Through the fretted stone I secretly observe the activities of all the little actors and stage hands going about their preparations. An inner fervor drives them as they set things up and watch them fall. Despite their ambitious attempts, the play never quite gets off the ground. The haveli owner says the children have been working all month on a segment of the 2000-year-old Ramayana epic written by the Anthill Sage, Valmiki.

"You know about Valmiki?"

"He was a bandit, tried to rob a holy man. But the holy man reproached him. 'Here, I give you a mantra. Repeat the name of Rama until you come clear.' Well, Valmiki mispronounced the mantra. He could not say Rama. It always came out Mara. He became obsessed with the mantra. He stayed in the forest just repeating things while a family of ants slowly built a hill over him. A dozen years passed. As soon as he stopped trying, the man was able to chant Mara back into Rama and underwent complete transformation. He became an enlightened sage. In the anthill he composed the Ramayana.

"All over India, night and day, somewhere part of this poem is being performed. If you don't see anything here, try another town. You'll catch a different episode, but you'll get the point. You can enter or exit the story anywhere. It is India's great gift to the world: the love poem of Rama and Sita, how the monster king abducts her and carries her off to his magic island. The king, of course, is the many-faced state of ignorance that kidnaps the mind with self-concern and deceit. It takes the patience and determination of Rama and the strength of his super-hero, the monkey Hanuman, to retrieve Sita. She is pure, unobstructed love, you know. And the evil king is really the enemy inside our own heads. The one that always has to be faced."

◈

Watching these children, it becomes obvious that the real drama is in the process, not in the end. It is in the innocent, spontaneous sense of the eternal present, the quickened energy of their whimseys. Two girls braid their hair with ribbons, wrap arrows with crepe, poke eyes in monster masks. A young lad sets up chairs, only to have a sudden twister race through the alley and topple them. A musician readies his tin-can drums on a wooden crate, waiting for a troupe of actors to appear from behind a curtain, only to have the curtain collapse, actors struggling beneath it, a stray cow wandering in to lick glue from the props. But these misfortunes do not cause anger. Through it all the children retain a sense of humor, a delight in the world as it is—with its collisions, follies, stray animals and tricks of fate.

Such attitude reminds me of a culture far from this one. A place where I worked once. The Eskimos in their Arctic desert. A cold afternoon on a frozen river. Children pretending to ice fish while their elders were off doing the real thing. In forever falling-down blanket-tents, the kids would drop imaginary lines into a mythical hole where who knows what waited. Quietly, as if silence was the most active response one could give in such an empty world, they took perch over the hole.

Suddenly, a great cheer . . .

Someone had just fished up a monkey! No ordinary monkey. But a monkey with wings, like Hanuman. "Manny," they called him. "Like man." The best thing about Manny was that he was invincible. Adults couldn't capture him. His was the power of flight, of turning invisible, of bounding from undersea to above land. Whereas big people couldn't see him, little ones could. For the rest of the afternoon, Manny was their playmate, their valiant model.

And this drama of the children of Jaisalmer?

Even in the face of total obliteration—dust scattering nylon wings and bamboo swords, cows eating cardboard storks and paper gazelles—the children of Jaisalmer share a hearty joy. They take glory in the high art of collapse. No adults override them with demands or suggestions in the form of short-tempered commands. As a voyeur from my third-story window I occupy a front seat to a High Mass in which each child is an acolyte. As evening falls and the lamps are lit, a realization enters me: that the real and underlying intent of any honest religion should be to return one to the idea of the great within the small, the sacred in the every day, the self not bowing to a distant god, but exuberant with "big joy" . . . the exalted, immediate, uncomplaining fervor of these kids at play in Jaisalmer.

※

THE DANCE OF WATERBIRDS AT KEOLADEO

e endless swirls of a snake's
alf-transparent dream beauty.
sh forming the Keoladeo Bird
efuge for over 350 species of

an emerald-breasted kingfisher
e bund I witnessed the solemn
cove, heard the musical chatter
hoopoe become twice its size,
:ket of morning glories.

ts overwhelming, I retreated to a
monk-like cell inside a government tourist bungalow in the center of the
refuge. The main decor, other than wash basin, pitcher, table and bed, was
a fat lizard who winked unmovingly during the day, fed nocturnally on
insects and returned to its zazen position on the wall at dawn. Meals were
taken in a small dining hall where signatures from travelers and
ornithologists from Beijing to Auckland garnered the register. Each of
these travelers left something behind: a monograph on the Siberian tern,
magazines from Paris, a toothbrush from Naples, dated newspapers from
Calcutta, Japanese romance novels, books on endangered species—and a
faded paperback by Robinson Jeffers. The latter I claimed, and spent
many candle-lit hours with it under the mosquito net while the lizard
moved happily around the room catching flies. A particular passage stood
out:

We must uncenter our minds from ourselves;
We must unhumanize our views a little, and become confident
As the rock and ocean that we were made from.

This particularly Taoist viewpoint came from a man who lived and
worked in solitude along the steep cliffs of California's Asia-facing Big
Sur coast. A man deeply immersed in the creative quietude basic to Zen
philosophy and ecology. He walked the silent fog-shrouded coves, built a
stone tower and filled his notebook as the sun sank between sheaves of
silvered mist. His words deepen our sense of unity with nature. His
poetry dwarfs us so that we become properly aligned with the "Dark
scant pasture drawn thin / Over rock shaped like flame." With him, we
find a hawk's egg in its secret nest, watch Antares redden in a rift of
cloud, and realize that we must make "kindlier music," that "the age
needs renewal."

The uncentering Jeffers celebrates became the core of my experience at
Keoladeo. Paddling across the bund was to become very small, a brush
stroke of a figure inked between scrolls of shadowy ripples and floating
lily pads. The atmosphere filled with cries and wingflap of waterfowl.
Ibis, spoonbills, egrets, darters, herons. Silhouetted in the late-afternoon
light, Siberian cranes formed calligraphic circles after a long
cross-continental flight. Watching them, I remembered myself as a
teenager reading Lawrence Ferlinghetti to the all-night medley of a
suburban mockingbird. Hidden deep in one of his famous longwinded
jazz-rambling poems were lines that spoke to this very moment:

I invented the alphabet
after watching the flight of cranes
who made letters with their legs ...

Here I was witnessing that same flight, those outstretched necks, the braking wings and dangling legs. Alphabet origins. Quick penbrush abstractions against the solar tide. Intricate designs incised in sculptured stone 50,000 years ago. The beginnings of song and dance. Strange utterances, brilliant sheen of feathers. Creatures with their own systems of memory, language and intelligence.

What place had I among them?
Spoiler. Waster. Overpopulator of the earth . . .

There were moments of true contemplation among those birds and rippling waters. And moments not of contemplation but of enormous vacancy. Body in raft glittering with reflected light. Eternity whirling, yet everything immaculate, serene. Flesh and soil with identical smells. Millions of insects marking the air in the setting sun. Millions of stars livening the sky as the atmosphere bled yellow-violet to indigo. Universe without weight of matter! Only floating silence of wooden raft through blood-dark inlets of the bund. A return into, and out from, the mysterious point of birth within the womb.

One evening, I joined Mr. Sham, the young ornithologist and part-time caretaker of Keoladeo, for a meal in the dining hall. We ate without silverware. Rice, curry, pickled mango served on banana leaves. Melancholy and withdrawn, he briefed me on the sanctuary's history.

"All of this was once private estate, a shooting preserve established by the local Maharaja for personal use. After the British left India the raja was stripped of power. The government made the swamp a national park. First, for the birds. And second, to give visitors a sense of spiritual well being. Such a burden of people in India! But here is one small area on a huge continent where we can find solace."

As Mr. Sham spoke, my eyes kept returning to the small pistol he unstrapped from his waist before dinner.

"There are problems with management here. Conflicts between locals struggling for daily survival and outsiders like me sent to preserve the park and its wildlife. Villagers poach trees for fuel, shoot cranes, kill deer, drive cattle into the swamp, pollute the food chain. I see no compromise. Occasionally they organize and gang up on professionals sent to band the birds and keep track of them. Locals never had a say in the raja's decision to convert their grazing lands into a swamp. Nor the government's decision to preserve it as a bird refuge.

"It is an old feud. Villagers despise government plans to stock the bund with fish to supplement their diet. For reasons of tradition they hate fish! They prefer their cows—for dung, for milk. And they complain bitterly about a government plan to seed the marsh with rice. The bund could have gates and waterways to control irrigation. With nets to protect the rice from the birds, everyone could live in harmony. But the villagers do not approve. They are lazy. They do not want to walk in detours around the bund to get to the planting area. They want to ruin the sanctuary with roads."

The ornithologist flicked his cigarette ashes onto the floor, poured hot tea from cup to saucer to cool it and sipped with downcast eyes.

"You and I can afford to enjoy this beauty. We come and go, tied to cash economy. These locals subsist on less per month than what you spent on your room last night. It is easy to become depressed about this. While we philosophize the villagers are out there shooting another deer. To let them have the refuge without compromise would certainly mean the end of the woods, the water and the animals. It has been proven all over India, all over the world. These resources cannot be replaced again. Shoot a white heron? We might as well shoot a classical court dancer. That is my opinion!

"We have strayed far off course. When I said Keoladeo is a sanctuary for birds as well as to restore the well being of our own spirit, I was not speaking superficially. Here, I can retreat from that huge, agitated India out there which refuses to examine itself. India! Always hiding behind busy nepotism, family, rituals, politics, bombings. We just are not ourselves anymore. If we are to surpass our woes and inadequacies, we must submit to the miracle of nature, the lessons of interdependence. In this awareness lies our renewal.

"If I had the power I would bring back Emperor Ashoka, India's pacifist king—third century B.C.—a Buddhist convert who rebelled against the warrior class he was raised in. He had forests reseeded, medicinal plants and banyan trees planted near wayside shrines, historical sites preserved, pillars erected and carved with Buddhist stories. Wildlife was studied and the hunting of threatened species forbidden. Animal sacrifices were out. But now where are we?

"Indians are blind to India. No interest in looking back, in learning from history. The rush is forward. To stop, to observe, to make judgments shakes the entire social ritual. Here, solitude affords a good look at what disturbs me, the systemization that tyrannizes me. I try to comprehend the whole picture. Define my position in the world rather than let society define me."

Paddling into the bund for the last time, I wrapped myself in a cotton blanket to ward off dawn's chill. A marvelous flight of waterbirds rose slowly above a spiraling line of amber mist. Mr. Sham sat opposite me, also wrapped tightly. We were quiet for a long time, until finally the young man—riddled with questions, resistant to the monstrous society beyond Keoladeo—spoke:

"What do we realize out here? That we are not the brains of the universe. Just cells that form part of its thinking."

In my silence I nodded, watching the birds, thinking—yes, only a part. No greater, no smaller than anything else joined in the temporal dance that spins us—like the exotic Asian Roller's aerial acrobatics—into the Taoist painter's brush, and out again onto the ephemeral canvas of the Divine.

▧

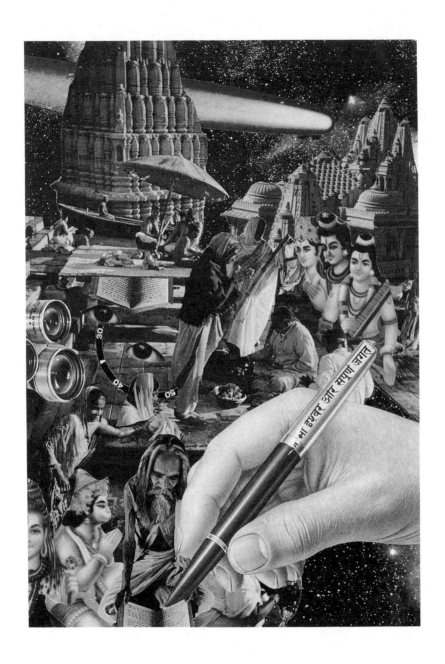

BHAYAANAK, A CINEMATIC DAYDREAM

Frail inheritance of sky. Surge of flesh below. A thin, white orb stumbling through the soot of high noon. From the upper story of the Time Tunnel Hotel, my eye becomes a lens of a creature not wholly of the world above nor of the one below. The ceiling fan squeaks and wobbles, its noise and feeble draft only intensifying the heat. Like ants in anarchy, aimless pedestrians overflow from one greasy doorway to another, maneuvering between jammed automobiles, sidestepping open sewers belching rotten drain water. Above the alleys loom the ubiquitous Indian movie posters. Plywood frames ten feet tall, gessoed and painted with garish men in suits and ties; buxom women with giant eyes and sequined waists curved like classic Ajanta cave paintings. Pretty women. Vulnerable and complying. The men, in contrast, are unshaven, deliberately brazen, baring open neckties and hairy chests—huge cubist cutouts flashing stylized grins, clutching briefcases, revolvers, important papers and keys.

Below the billboards, the curb sweepers take a smoke break, the rat removers have long ago finished their nightly rounds, the perfume vendors empty their morning earnings into wooden boxes, the blood donors squat and compare needle marks. They gather near the old British-style government building, an imposing structure festering like a gray sore with unhappy tax payers. Anxiety. Grief. Servitude. Porous dream of humanity bound for nowhere, smoldering like a compost heap in the derelict sun.

I look down, the eternal voyeur, into a flimsy web of neighborhoods where each citizen is a refugee in a hot-wired jumble of extended families doing their best under sagging electric lines and rusty tin roofs. Ferment of confusion, snarl of poverty—they are framed in my eye like a darkened miniature. My window frame is painted bright yellow, outlining a darkened composition of tiny people aged with soot and red caste marks, whiplash of history, handbags of garlic and aubergine. They run, stand still, holler, bow, chatter, sip hot milk, spit foil wrappings from sweets, perch, unfurl white cotton, wash, spit, urinate, coil, pray, scatter in fast forward, reverse in slow motion and crane their necks up, way up, to the looming movie stars. Then, ever curiously, they nod heads as if to agree—first with the men and women on the posters, then with each other—that these bigger-than-life stars are clearly the elected officials that represent their hidden dreams, private lusts and ultra-secret fantasies.

BHAYAANAK the billboards read.

Bombay's latest film hit. A cinematic daydream invading Hindu lifestyle with all the jive and promiscuity of the Christian West. The film typifies thousands of other movies cranked out by Bombay's dozens of studios responsible for the production of over 500 films annually. In the majority of them it is the male who is the go getter, outspoken with his desires and achievements; possessed with heraldic notions and tear-jerking laments. With his briefcase, busy schedule, shiny automobile, lethal pistol, fat wallet and scrolls of floorplans, he is the symbol of technology, industrialization and unwavering machismo.

The woman is down lower. She cannot fix her own dreams. The man is there, big-shouldered and outspoken, to fix them for her. Her business is to remain on her knees. Pleading. Continually putting herself in the position to please or to listen. Preferably she never interrupts the man's schedule with her own laments and problems. She doesn't speak. She obeys. She gives. She bends to pick up a fallen order, shows a sultry cleavage and two scenes later is raped, her sari peeled away as the audience bites its nails. Then, for reasons of censorship, the director cuts to a close up of a boiling locomotive. Its lubricated pistons pump into action. Smoke bellows from its hot lungs. Cut again. An outdated standup ashtray teeters and falls to the floor. The rapist's smoldering cigarette sets the woman's sari afire. The screen is covered with dramatic orange flames. Behind the flames: a brief and extremely blurred glimpse of a couple impossibly tangled on a sagging bed.

The billboards are amusing at first. Ten seconds later, painful. I stare at them, they stare back. Underneath their scaffolding, India writhes. Bombay influences the dress of the upper class, the look of the deities, the actions, mutinies, sexual tensions of the mob, the tough-guy stance and nail-file murders of street gangs, the ubiquitous need to pin women down, to hold them in submissive roles, to unfurl the wet silk from their hips (always the evocative "monsoon scene" where the maiden's rain-drenched sari reveals every sensuous cleft and curve of the torso) and passionately deflower them while the deities, framed in plastic, look on.

In a country where religious demands never end, where the entire nervous system has for millennia been invaded by bells, incense, *puja* and the chatter of overweight priests, these movie heroes—their irresponsibility, the seeming ease with which they break rules and control fate—seem to fill a place of psychic longing in every citizen. One can abandon faith in the darkness of the movie hall. Leave ritualism behind. Cut the cord to the ancient past. Let the teachings blur, the gods become alien.

Eventually, I retreat from my window, the bars of pink neon, the sequined lettering, the pointed breasts and fake smiles. Naked on the bed, staring into the center of the ceiling fan, I see the words **EASY ROTATION WORKS   EASY ROTATION WORKS   EASY ROTATION WORKS** printed on the chrome eye where the blades meet. A thump at the door arouses me. I open it—to the sound of quickly disappearing footsteps.

Empty corridor . . .

Closing the door, I notice a series of peepholes drilled through the wood at various levels, and upon further examination—outside the door on my knees—discover that most of the peepholes are drilled to line up precisely with the level of the bed. How many innocent travelers had been caught in the act of love or after-shower nudity by the starved eyeballs of the hotel's crew?

❊

Morning arrived. Darkness gave way to an unkept city, flattened layers of rubbish, fumy grit pressed to the asphalt. Eyeglasses, hair, shoes, skin: the grime of exhaust covered everything. I chose a peephole and caught an early-morning bloodshot eye already there watching me. I waited awhile, opened the door and stared in reverse pinhole effect to my own sad belongings on the mattress. Like it or not, I was a participant in the human movie. India was a country of voyeurs, one spying upon another. Not for a moment was there relief from the endless video: Indian streets, Indian billboards above the streets, Indian peepholes in the door, India that mushroomed through sleep at night and refused to shut off by day. The false props above the city only heightened the idea of voyeurs. They were frightening, they haunted my reality, those plywood actors scanning their doubles on the pavement.

The city was a tidal wave crashing down with centuries of build up, a wall of thick water submerging the traveler with debris of collapsed domes, scalloped arches, tantric altars, murky sewers, ribboned carriages, a horse wired with light bulbs, a monkey twirling around its legless master, beggar projected upon Brahmin, Muslim upon Hindu, dung lady upon landlord, the ex raja stuffing his face with *barfi,* the sadhu sleeping on cactus pads. Faces, feet, dialects, costumes, bald heads, torsos, turbans, bulls, parrots, teething babies, latrine washers, acrobats, biers of garbage, biers of corpses, police wagons, circus nets, pelvises, pendants, farmers, bakers, shadowboxers, the prostitute wringing out her red underwear, the missionary picking his pimples, the heretic, the little guy in satin shreds with heehawing voice, the pregnant woman selling pesticides, the fathead with trays of cotton wicks and imported licorice: they overlapped with translucent shadows. Each and every drama was splashed upon the senses, lithographed off-register. The big dividing line between rich and poor, the obvious distribution of wealth between "clean" and "unclean"—it all became obvious as one strolled into the wretchedness of the city.

Pavement sleepers, slum dwellers crowded sixteen to a 20x20 flat, servants lined up to pay morning tribute to an oily monster giving orders from his porch. If one could find a private space to plan, there might be mutiny. But there was no revolution, no quiet moment to scheme. There was hunger, and the idea of fate, destiny. The underprivileged lived in crowded cells made only of wire netting for walls. Tension, squabbles—they were inevitable. Screams. Ghetto smoke. Quarreling families numbed by toil and ceremony. Pressure. Graft. Asbestos ceilings. Blue walls lit by 40-watt bulbs. Conflict. Acceptance. Over-sweet incense smoldering above stinking tanning yards.

In "The Colony," upper class Indian men in polo shirts and pin-striped shorts played badminton. The women, dressed in the manner of their British colonizers, basked on white lawnchairs and grew obese on *gulab jamun*. Milk sweets. Little figurines of upperclass dough served in Dravidian syrup. They gossiped softly while the necessary murders were performed. In both the hierarchy and the lower caste, a deeper rage was hidden by religion. Duty, performance, paying homage, doing puja was to deny thought or examination. Through them the worshiper was kept at a safe distance from himself, planted in front of mannequin-like, plastic gods and goddesses dressed in modern attire, coiffed like movie-stars.

⌗

Torn sunlight through coal vapors. The stairway outside my room descends into a green-cement courtyard where women bend over knotted piles of soggy laundry and freshly-rinsed bedpans upside down in a row under sheet-and-towel verandas. Baba Yama, the hotel manager whose hairy navel protrudes like an obscene penis through a large tear in his dirty undershirt, draws a long drag on his bidi, waves, then scolds the child servants coughing in the wet courtyard. I exit into the frenzy of India's streets, instantly transformed into another anonymous victim of the celluloid asylum.

The eternal hack is everywhere. Untouchables on hands and knees clean spittle marks from pillars and sidewalks. As fast as they wash the sputum, it reappears. As they stroll, men's mouths well with red liquid. Lime paste and cardamom. Nuts and spices wrapped in betel leaves. It drips down chins, onto *dhotis*, and spurts like blood sacrifice between every syllable they speak. To meet a *pan*-chewer is like running into someone whose teeth have just been knocked out in a gang war.

54

BHAYAANAK . . .

A billboard sparkled with thousands of aluminum sequins high above the streets—the only thing clean appearing in the whole dreaded chaos. Under it I stood dwarfed. If not spied upon through my bedroom door, I was looked down upon by these cinematic gods who unfurled their silks and daggers over the pavement's bleak grime. Or, climbing aboard a rickshaw, I found myself riding above those same heroes. Their replicas painted in miniature on fenders and axles. A golden-eyed Garuda gliding through puffy-pink airbrushed clouds. Lovers in convoluted postures behind huge lotus leaves with Baby Krishna looking on. Sappy half nudes on white stallions meeting mid stream in a paradise of blue stone and crimson fern.

Through narrow arteries thick with chatter I became lost, submerged in mingled soundtracks, broken-record cries, prerecorded hawkers' litanies scratchy with dust and fingerprints. Every intersection was a canyon fork, a crossing of human streams. The pestering was unending. It began in English and ended in Hindi. I bought a pocket dictionary of phrases, *Hindustani Without a Master.* But it was outdated, of no practical use, prepared by some British colonial dunce in the 1930s. A page titled "Useful Phrases" read:

"Come near me
    Stand still
      Clean my room
        Can you write in English?
       You are very lazy
     Bring me my clothes
      Undress me
        These are not my collars

<pre>
                    I want to wash
             You have burnt these clothes
               Tighten the harness
            Oil it, lather it
Pump up!"
</pre>

�֎

The doors of the State Bank were open. The place looked cool. I walked in. Men sat behind wooden desks dressed in cream-colored tunics, holy marks on their foreheads, a few in pressed shirts and ties, maroon and mustard color combinations. The floor was marble, little piles of dust and rags and feathers swept into the corners. High ceilings. Muted sunlight filtering through frosted windows set inside tall hardwood arches.

I was hoping to refresh myself, change some travelers checks, sip a paper cup of "Filter Boiled Ice Water" from the dispenser next to the tellers' cage, but what I walked into was yet another Indian movie. The closer my feet took me the more I realized the decrepit state of the edifice. Paint was peeling from the pillars. Great chunks of the monsoon-logged ceiling had fallen to the floor. Squares of glass were missing from the windows. Doves nested between the dirty crystal of a broken chandelier. A sign on the wall read:

TIME IS GOLD DO NOT FRITTER IT AWAY

I approached the tellers' cage. No one. On the floor behind old mahogany desks, between confused ledgers and hopelessly-entwined scrolls of adding-machine tape, the clerks sat cross legged. They were barefoot, shuffling cards, smoking bidis. The bank clock above them was stopped with its hands straight up. An official with kernals of rice decorating his eyebrows, a stubby beard and diaper-like wraps, stuffed a quid of pan in his mouth and crouched to inspect a busted typewriter. Another, in identical dress, stamped and restamped endless voucher forms. One more hunkered over a sooty pressure lamp, pumping and priming it.

No time on the clock. No one at the tellers' cage. No electricity. I took a seat. Fifteen minutes, half an hour passed. In my palm I held a brass token. Behind the marble counters my passport lay in a mess of unfinished paperwork. Ditto, the two twenty-dollar travelers checks I wished to cash. But the bank was cool. And obviously void of the frenzied pace on the streets outside.

I looked around. fifteen feet up in the wall in front of me was a niche where Ganesha beamed a tusked smile. A crimson swastika was fingerpainted on his belly. Plastic flowers and a wilted yellow candle adorned the shrine. Unconsciously I fiddled with the brass token, moving it from one hand to the other. An hour passed. Two men with a ladder arrived, placed the ladder against the wall under Ganesha, and left. A funeral parade passed outside. A bank clerk noticed my shifting posture on the lobby bench.

"Suffering?" he asked. "All of us are suffering here."

A few more minutes and the electricity suddenly switched on. Adding machines everywhere began to clack and shift gears, adding spontaneous tape to the coils already flowing between the desks. Lopsided piles of forms and thin sheets of carbon fluttered wildly beneath glass paperweights as ceiling fans started up by themselves at full speed. The doves defecated from their chandelier and flew out the door. The two men who brought in the ladder returned, each carrying a banana and smoking incense sticks up the ladder to Ganesha's shrine. At last the day was in order. The god had been honored. The bank was ready to close.

Another twenty minutes, five or six forms and several signatures later, I received my passport back, handed over the brass token, moved from window number three to window number five to window number one, signed another carbon slip, watched the cashier slowly open a battered money box, sort through a mass of wrinkled bills, and begin counting them one by one—ironing them with his hands, holding them to the light to check their watermarks. It was then I noticed another aphorism neatly printed and framed under glass:

DELAY CAUSES CORRUPTION

Late afternoon. City thick with smoke and sweat. Near the depot, two trucks try squeezing through a tunnel at the same time. Into the darkness they pass, and out comes an elephant, spray-painted bronze and green. On its back a man sits tangled in electrical wires, yelling through a microphone that only occasionally functions. He is advertising a circus. On one side of the elephant is a placard of a naked woman sticking her head into the mouth of a lion. On the other, a mustached man in a shiny magician's hat sawing a princess in half.

Now comes the abrupt and penetrating sound of three men in breechcloths, their locks of hair and balls and buttocks madly shaking as they work jackhammers—tearing apart an old garden wall. Through the debris a camel appears, hauling a massive tree trunk, sap bleeding from its freshly-sawed end. From an open apartment window a mother holds out her naked baby who arches a stream of urine into a row of potted plants.

Back toward the Time Tunnel Hotel the streets narrow again. Pundits seated high on alleyway thrones sprinkle marigolds upon passing women carrying curried peas wrapped in banana leaves. As if to imitate the attire of the film stars on the billboards high above, a parade of children adorned in mock turbans and throw-away rags—with beards, eyebrows and beauty marks painted with mud—appear suddenly from between bamboo scaffolding. They move along the gloomy shop fronts like a glittering, supernatural island, a collection of floating debris barked at and chased by dogs. With arms extended high, several of them hold aloft a wooden box with the remnants of a doll inside it, chanting:

"One baby hungry one chapati mama
     One baby hungry one chapati mama
          One baby hungry one chapati mama"

As if to deliberately mock the pathos of the scene, an advertisement is tacked to a concrete pillar in front of a dry good's store. The poster depicts two blond babies on a clean shag rug crawling up to a box of Glucose Biscuits.

What Are little girls made of?
Tears and dolls, frills and falls
And bubbling energy
          —from Glucose, the tasty energy food!

Past the shrouded sleepers in the Time Tunnel stairway, I climb. Back to the peepholes. The bed. The verandah. The view of the darkened city, the heightened anarchy of noise, the faceless essence, the supernatural halos of argon illuminating the billboards.

B H A Y A A N A K . . . . . on and off the lettering blinks.

"Bhayaanak," the hotel manager tries to explain, "means to be afraid, that there is danger all around."

Ten feet tall, a man with fluttering coattails is lit on the skyline. Seven feet tall, a woman with tongue licking her upper lip, breasts bulging from sequined vest, melts beneath him. I recline on top of a thin freshly-laundered sheet, pink curlicues of neon strobing my body, restless with sleep that will not come. Heat of memory, dust of illusion. Celluloid boundaries around the fractured dream. India the hunter. India the victim. Stage prop of body overlapping body borne upon the screen.

▨

JOURNEY TO LADAKH

Up through Hindu India, into Kashmir's Muslim world, the Separatist tensions, the Cease Fire Line between Pakistan and India, and over Zoji La. A frightening route twisting through the Himalayas into the arid moonscape of Leh—two miles high. This is Buddhist land, once part of Tibet, its scenery reminiscent of Death Valley, the Andes of Antofagasta or Utah's incredulous hoodoo country. Places where ethereal vistas dupe the mind, bamboozle the eye with raw edges of cliff that abruptly crumble into bottomless canyons. Each treeless rib of creation bleeds with mineral pinks, mint greens, ochre and lavender. Mirages hoodwink the senses. Roads tilt, trails disappear as you walk, shadows evaporate. Halt for a moment to get your bearings and the compass spins.

Near the cliff-perched monastery of Lamayuru the bus wobbles and shakes. I am squeezed against the cracked window in a broken seat of drugged-looking, head-nodding young conscripts with loaded rifles—military men from thousands of miles away, loosely bound by the Hindi language, en route to the high Himalayas where they'll build roads and guard the borders from China. My face is forced against the cold glass. A paroxysm overtakes me as I peer into a drop off with no end. The hard seat over the axle rattles my jaw. The battered bus carriage hangs over the wheels enough to convince me that I am not in a bus at all, but suspended in the hands of a madman operating a flimsy tram over the jaws of death. At night we pause in a canyon of wind-scoured crevasses, a Muslim shanty town with cranky innkeepers, reheated food, hard beds and contraband arms.

Next morning, in a biting breeze, the driver lights diesel-soaked rags under the engine to warm the crankcase. Nobody smiles as the bus rattles off in a puff of cold dust. The road, constructed at the cost of hundreds of Indian workers falling to their deaths, is a zigzag thread looped between massive peaks. A stone tossed over a cliff to test for bottom echoes no sound. The most immediate reaction is to weep. At one's insignificance. At the sheer power of creation. I am displaced by hemispheres, by strange languages and bizarre juxtaposition of religions: animist, Sikh, Islamic, Buddhist, Hindu. The landscape completes the disorientation: hallucinatory, surreal, a daydream mixed with psychic tangles, the body's electrons crazily rearranged. Open your eyes, there it is. Close your eyes, you can't escape. Fall into sleep and day fast forwards into night, an unceasing play of mirage and aftershock.

❈

Outside Leh, at Sonam Taishi's ample village house, I lodge. A modest two-story, flat roofed adobe near the Indus River. A bee-humming orchard. Tall, butter-yellow poplars lit like candles along hand-dug waterways, a few of them diverted into tiny mill houses to power the grinding stones. A small oasis in this high desert, and a good spot to rest, walk, witness and reflect.

Sonam Taishi is a middle-aged Ladakhi farmer, father of several grown children—married and single; traders, storekeepers and religious novices. Drinking endless cups of *solja*—Ladakhi tea—we warm our hands over a cast-iron cook stove fired with dung, eat puff bread baked right on the coals and converse best we can in broken English: about Tibetans in process of fleeing China, about the Dalai Lama's political position, about India's military stronghold on Ladakh. About tourism. Meditation. And about sound. For Sonam recites the Buddhist litanies, sings plow songs, planting songs, harvesting and threshing songs.

I relate to him my experience of seeing sound once, in the starry expanse of the Navajo badlands. On a moonless evening I sat up from sleep, awakened by coyotes—their singular cacophonous cries joined into a weird harmony that dropped suddenly into austere silence. Night was a great curved ceiling banded with scintillating auras which I could simultaneously perceive with the eye and hear with the ear. Audible waves: at first like distant shattering glass, then very close. Was it the starry night *sounding* the auras into existence, or the auras themselves *imaging* a chromatic, sonar presence into my eye?

Sonam believes that sound waves and "seen" waves are interchangeable. That when he chants a mantra he sees sound. Repeating a mantra gives way to visual vibrations as each syllable is called out. "You begin to see a shape, a seed, the beginning of life."

The body's mass is form given weight by moving particles of sound. Knowledge of flesh begins with the understanding of light. Between heaven and earth a shaman travels on rungs of sound, his body splintered into wave lengths of light. In the mantric tradition of Tibetan monks, voices harmonize, atoms dance in suspension, the body is returned to the universe in its original form.

Once, in the alleys of Old Delhi, a silk vendor flashed his scarves, demanding that I linger and look. The moiré patterns of the silks transfixed my eye as they billowed in the afternoon sun. From each sheen a sound oscillated forth in concentric circles: a ringing of kingfisher blue, pentatonic waves shimmering from maroon, prismatic rhythms of repeating symmetries from lilac and lemon yellow, a dazzle of chromatic

65

voices inside what I mistook to be pure white.

In the intermittent silence between speech at a silk-vendor's kiosk, or in the starry expanse above the Navajo badlands, one experiences the idea of creative sound revealed to us by Himalayan Rishis, the Seers of subtle forces within the universe. Dancing atoms perpetually speak from the inherent geometric patterns in all life. Put your ear to a rattlesnake's diamond design wrapped around its moving vertebrae, or to the geological rifts of a human palm, or inside the fibrous whorl around a silkworm's cocoon. Sound is there, the same kind that is replicated by those who know how to listen: the Zunis, with their trance-inducing chants; tribal Africa, with its rich textures of drumming; the Australian Aborigines, exhaling song through termite-hollowed trunks, or the Tibetan monks—their Tantric drone up from within the body's deep cave. All elevate mind as well as voice. All rise from an unconscious chemistry that crests inside the flesh and rolls from the tongue. All infuse the eye with labyrinths of sound transformed into light, mathematical imprints normally seen only under the most powerful electron microscope. The solitary vision quest of the Rishi, or the Sufi dervish seeding the air with mystic verse in ecstatic spin: here, too, the making of sound visible through a temporary displacement of the body into the primal matter of the cosmos.

▨

Many days have passed. This morning began like most mornings: Brueghal-like groups of villagers in fields; soft breeze rippling the sparkling curves of the Indus; men and boys driving oxen around threshing poles; girls winnowing grain and spreading it with wooden rakes; women in slow trot behind their sheep—talking low, twirling distaffs, dressed in sheepskin capes, upturned shoes, dark clothing and colorful aprons, rare stones around necks, flint boxes on woven sashes.

Much of my thinking has been replaced with doing. Winter is coming on, air crisp, chili pods drying on flat roofs, fresh coats of blue paint applied to window and door frames, jagged mountains waiting for snow. People need help with piling kindling wood, raking and bundling fodder. I can be of some aid, though plenty of the time finds me the object of curiosity, a form of entertainment. They live here; they'll stay. They'll suffer out the cold and get back to their low-sun-in-the-sky stories, their political and economic worries, their tasks at hand, their fears, joys, feuds, celebrations and quarrels. I'll go. Remain at length in solitude and decipher where I've been. Share with loved ones. Teach. Grow a garden. Perhaps travel elsewhere. Sonam's village has seen many of my kind come, stay awhile, observe with intrigue and vanish.

A Canadian traveler came by yesterday. We compared rucksacks. Mine was weighty, filled with books and stones. His was light, packed intimately with bright cloth. "Better to collect silk than stone," he laughed. Wrapped in the cloth was a book, ragged pages of verse by Tagore, which he left with me. A passage in it seems to sum up the pathos that has entered my thoughts lately:

We know people only in dotted outlines with gaps in our knowledge which we have to fill in ourselves. Those we know well are largely made up of our imagination. The lines are so broken, with even the guiding dots missing, that a portion of the picture remains darkly confused and uncertain. But perhaps it is these very loopholes, allowing entrance into each other's imagination, which make for intimacy.

Of this household I have a favorite. It is Sonam's twenty-year-old daughter, Bhuti, who is home from studies at Lamayuru to help with harvest. She is a Buddhist novice, hair shaved short, maroon garment permeated with smoke, a little white puppy dog in her arms much of the time, a big smile on her full, brown face. A reincarnate Bodhisattva, for sure. The very embodiment of joy. She's been filling the cellar with potatoes, sorting apricots, slicing them to dry on a flat rock behind the house. Each morning she knocks on my door with a steaming thermos of solja flavored with salt and yak butter. Then comes the freshly-baked puff breads, tasting of yesterday's ground wheat and a bit of charcoal from the stove. During the day Bhuti moves about with grace and quietness, maximizing every action with tenderness. Her world seems to be one of direct seeing, untampered by philosophy. Whether there are wicks to be trimmed or prayers to be recited, the dog to be fed or soil to be prepared—careful attention is given, without the mind in the way.

Through her I recall New Mexico's Pueblo women: the immediacy of their laughter, the knowing silence, the precise timing for words. While the men busy themselves with elaborate systems of ritual drama to explain creation, the women sweep clay ovens, prepare chili, store seeds for next season's planting in the symmetrical pots they fashion from clay. They know well the process of creation. Like the graceful vessels guarding their seeds, their bodies hold this knowledge: the cycle of pregnancy and labor, the opening of birth.

Two nights ago Bhuti motioned that I should enter the little chamber where she was busy block-printing prayer flags. A remarkable experience occurred. One that brought me back to conversations with Sonam: his ideas on mantra and sound, of the magic of the world at hand. The state of infanthood, where you are seeing and hearing the world for the first

68

time—no separation between audio and visual.

By candle flame, seated with Bhuti on the stone floor, I watched her hands deftly roll lampblack over her spirit-horse woodblocks and press squares of green and yellow cotton cloth to the carvings. Her eyes beamed as she removed each prayer flag from the inked blocks. The backwards gallop on the wood was now a lively forward gallop on the cloth. For a long time we sat immersed in the process, unspeaking. Then, through her brother—himself barely able to speak English—she asked my name. In the darkness I hesitated. Should the silence be broken? Before more consideration passed, each letter of my name began to erupt in spontaneous fusion from way within my body. Assembled at the tip of the tongue, they took flight:

"*J o h n . . .*"

I spoke without knowing I spoke. And saw those letters, the *sound* of each one, become visible atoms in the pores of night. And knew that Bhuti saw too. A smile from her eye, then the sudden disappearance of that flaming calligraphy. In night's womb, in that emotional vibration of primeval light, in that mystic spiral of sound that must have existed before creation, I heard my name for the very first time . . .

Visible sound, and the awakening of my flesh to that sound.
Metaphysics of sound. My self given another dimension through sound.

❋

BEFORE DAYBREAK, VARANASI

A dream, a prop, a stage, this city. Ancient when Buddha arrived to turn the Wheel of Dharma. Ancient, today, under the blazing zodiac before dawn. The skyline is a cardboard cutout: tilted, spired, domed, boiling over with monstrous heads of banyans whose tangled roots coil downward from gnarled limbs, pulverizing the moist stone of the old temples that nursed them into existence. Above, the moon hangs as if on wires, foiled with gold, backed by a frayed black cloth.

What moves? Only the nodding trees in the starry breeze. The rats. And slithering shapes of ghost-like *harijans*—the untouchables—meandering the sidewalks, hired by city officials to spread lines of phosphorescent lye to decontaminate the gutters. Through narrow alleys along the riverfront they slink, down the *ghats* leading into the thick waters of the Ganges. There, they disappear between bobbing houseboats, the freshly-painted tourist gondolas, the dank mangers of moaning water buffaloes whose undereaves hold sleeping crows.

The old city lifts and lowers, a moored hulk, flame lit and creaking in its black harbor. Its captain is missing, its anchor heavy—a somnolent eye weighted with barnacles, the unpronounceable names of countless divinities, thick books of heroic tragedies. Along forked passageways the puppet man sleeps, a wart curer wraps himself in the arms of the bangle lady, a shoeshine boy clatters out a wheezing cough. A lone star plummets from the darkness. Each alley bears sharp odors of destitute human bodies layered in dark geologic strata. Restless snoring bodies turned green in the brassy night. Toppled pieces of Giocometti sculpture. Orphans, widows,

71

sannyasins waiting to die at the Ganges, to be free of the spinning rebirth wheel.

The aged, the wandering, the baggy-balled ones, the whimpering infants, grandmothers with grey breasts knotted like rope: all shiver together in half sleep. Under a stone peacock, three astrologers wrestle with their dreams. One has a missing eye, its scar uncovered, skin tissue knitted together in the shape of a star. Next to him coils a rat-faced beggar born without vertebrae. His everyday ritual is to slide aboard a castor-wheeled plank and balance an alms bowl on his bony chest in front of the city bank. Next to the beggar sleeps a thin street mother, her face plastered with healing leaves. At her side a tiny baby clicks its tongue and lifts a frail ribcage. Its fists open as if to grasp something in a nightmare. A tiny orphan, perhaps. Abandoned because she disappointed her father by being a girl. Over everyone, a stone goddess presides. Her breasts are blackened with incense, her vulva fingerprinted with thousands of supplications. Her bulging eyes are vacuous and unblinking as they rotate to oversee the sleepers.

Nothing is understandable.

The world isn't created to make sense. A bull grazes in someone's living room where bony disciples clang finger cymbals and wail a cheerless mantra full of whining pleas in front of a foggy-eyed guru. At his feet there's an ancient black telephone, its receiver off the hook. God is a fable in the darkness. One has to sidestep human excrement to pray at his altar. Or dodge the suffering Hindu who whips himself with cactus pads while standing upside down like an inverted Babylonian tower.

Through a pair of blue shutters comes the parchment-thin voice of a young bride whimpering under the weight of her man. While she submits there comes an amplified splatter of someone urinating down the alley. Dawn. The ubiquitous movie billboards snicker with larger than life smiles. The bride cries. At the Cantonement Station a steam train echoes her scream with a piercing whistle: a hollow sound disfiguring the air, the trees, the brassy temples slanting into the Ganges. The sky wants to lighten but can't. The bride wants to remove herself from the weight of her groom but can't. Her legs struggle under the urge of his body, under the noisy snore of his relatives in the next room, under the thickness of the city—its oily air pressing down like the heavy pages of a soiled book.

The modern Varanasi is equal to the old. Top heavy with the same victims of caste and kings and dogmatic priests that inspired Buddha's revolt centuries ago. Varanasi is brown upon brown, a crumbling monastery bobbing helplessly in a fouled harbor, leaking on all sides but never going under. A huge eyeball turned in on itself. A spoiled nirvana waterlogged in a murk of prayers and assemblies and bombed voting stalls. The straining thighs, the nests of scavenger birds eating the eyes of floating corpses, the scribe lifting his pen from a nightmare, the underclass and the kings, they are still here.

The world wears a mask. Its wise men are forced onto crutches. Giant amplifiers sputter Vedic hymns into the ears of the innocent. But the prophets' books are kept under lock and key in museums, or buried under movie theaters where heroines bleat like goats and muscle men fire sawed-off shotguns. Down Dasaswamedh Lane a mendicant is scraped from the pavement, hit by a milk truck after years of pilgrimaging to get here. No matter. He came to die. It was to be the high point of a his life to expire in this city. Varanasi's industry is death.

✖

With the sky's first brightening the streets become an impossible tangle of nerve endings. A sudden multitude of devotees crowds every inch of pavement like a sheet of flame. Everyone heads toward the river, each carrying a towel, tiny brass bucket, toothbrush, flowers, prayer beads, a tray of bones or bag of a relative's ashes.

The sun's yoke splits to reseed the world. Yellow drips from the sky, over the face of a mad woman crying from her padded cart. A barber's blade shaves the already-bald head of a meditating Brahmin. Silver talismans glint from a naked boy's penis. In every direction people amble off to pray or defecate in the morning sunrise. In pairs they gossip while ridding their bowels, laughingly sticking their heads between legs to inspect the shape and color of what they've digested.

At Manikarnika Ghat a sooty courtyard is filled with gnarled firewood—a sea of broken ships, cursed islands, black bones of dinosaurs. The low-caste *doms*—funeral attendants—carry the wood to giant scales where merchants weigh and sell it to destitute funeral parties hardly able to bear the cost. If they can't pay for a proper load, their loved one will only half burn, then be dumped into the river to float toward the Bay of Bengal. The greasy merchants move arrogantly. Their fingers are ornamented with gold, their pomaded hair stuck with ashes from cremation pyres along the shore. The distraught funeral parties shell out precious rupees, fits of rage beneath their remorse. The merchants' eyes remain disengaged, bright with power. The doms heap the wood into crisscrossed stacks, place the corpses on them and ignite the bodies. One by one they blaze, like fiery votive lamps.

All day, all night long. They blaze . . .

One body raises its arms, all ten fingers aflame like candles. Another corpse is almost gone, its flaming heart enshrined by glowing ribs, leg bones folded backwards into the pyre by the attendants who shield their faces from the writhing heat. Smoke and ash churn upward, round and round, rising in hazel spirals, veiling the sun so that it becomes blurred and bloated: a whirling eye in the center of India's ancient, wheeling swastika. An eye peering into the hearts, mouths and faces of mourners. An eye blinking at the defecating men on the beach. An eye with tears at its corners. For the lepers struggling beneath firewood. For the ashen funeral attendants wielding huge poles, slamming them into the heads of the burning bodies to release their trapped spirits.

No abstract death here. No philosophical idea. No flowered and embalmed smiling body in metal casket preserved for well-dressed church goers. Only matter turned to vapor, everything once human recycled back into the universe. A fluttering, diaphanous alphabet of carbon, water and liquid heat falling as ash into the city sewers, the open yonis, the soup bowls and lotus ponds, the knotted turbans of limping warriors, and down, down through the resinous cracks of the bedbug shanties.

※

A burro yawns.
A tern battles with a raven.
A naked sadhu rides the bow of a dilapidated raft, his body smeared with cow dung. A tourist boat glides by, bannered and perfumed. Its cargo is manicured. Each person holds a long lens to capture the city, its minarets, the sadhu, the burning pyres. The river is safe. The powerful motor of the

boat drones out the smells and sounds of the dying. The foreigners eat their sack lunches and point, point to everything. And from everywhere a finger points back. The finger is connected to something living, yet somewhere unfinished, beyond itself. It is connected to the phantom of India. A phantom still waiting for its body to arrive.

❈

How many fill the streets today?
How many into the fire tomorrow?

Look—on the steps of the Ganges—a spider boy all deformed: half human, half monkey, dancing his futile dance while tourists heave coins and crows swoop to steal his pay. And there, half in the river, her sari tucked into her crotch, is the bride of darkness in the full blaze of day washing away her groom's seed while, in the sand beneath a pyre, a dog gives birth to a litter of puppies.

Varanasi . . .

Slow tide of fire. Jackal that bends on hands and knees. Eye of the goddess, eye of the dream inside the clairvoyant flower. Language of shadows, leaves, smoldering pyres. Language of naked priests over naked infants in cardboard boxes on the river shore. Awnings covered with ash. Street upon street transparent with desire. Shrine upon shrine smeared with blood and *ghee*. River of rivers. City of cities subdividing with the designs of life into a cosmogram of light.

❈

A QUESTION OF JOURNEY

Here comes the sun . . .

The Beatles play from a tape deck on a window ledge overlooking the city's curdled bowl of citizens. Two stories below, the loonies, the fruit peelers, the wiry consumptives gather to hear *bhajan* melodies, live, from a circle of naked men seated on scraps of cardboard. I brew strong coffee on a tiny Optimus stove, and stare from the open doorway which exits from my guest room onto a sagging balcony.

Like the magic tablets mother once dropped into a bowl of water at my childhood bedside, Varanasi has sprouted overnight into a crystalline maze profuse with pagodas and ruffled towers. Through them explodes the morning sun—a sun quite unlike the sun in any other part of the world: a brass gong lifting slowly through dust, smoke and hundreds of sadly-puffing locomotives, each with a mystical star on its nose. Over the Ganges the orb swells, crimson to hammered gold to fluorescing white, heating my nerve endings as I survey the city from the balcony.

Two stories below, the market in the narrow *gulli* has been active since dawn—a penumbra of prayer and thievery, glistening brass and dirty jewels. Astrologers unpack their charts from canvas satchels and take charge of the day. As the sun rises the mob intensifies, surging like murky rapids through the dark canyon filled with mended awnings and relentless hawkers. Then, out of the darkness the heads bob—into a shabby city block where an old rusty circus wheel dominates a makeshift carnival. But the electricity has failed. The wheel has quit turning. Nervous mothers, stopped in mid air, clutch their wide-eyed babies. In bright breeze-rippled saris, the women look like a mandala of stained glass against the sky. As they relax and begin to gabble loudly from various points on the wheel, their gold fillings flash in the sun.

I let it all enter, hand moving with nacreous spirals in my journal as the eyes glance up and center on a young boy standing in his mother's lap. At the very crest of the circus wheel he seems king of a ragtag world, glad for the power failure, content to be inspecting the chaos below from his swinging bucket of a throne.

Like a whirlpool pulling you into its vortex, Varanasi dissolves all distance between seer and seen. Eyes jump from their sockets into a pandemonium so intense that angles, textures, faces, riotous colors oscillate with such fury as to become a motionless abstraction. A Jackson Pollock drip painting. A rare postage stamp magnified out of proportion where, within its perimeters, one discovers a few lines hidden by Rimbaud; a cat born with a dog's face; a blubbery eunuch sweeping the entrance to a palace slowly sinking as the Ganges gnashes its sandy teeth against its foundation.

Here, tipsy displays of second-hand dentures promise smiles full of teeth. Here, lips fall from faces in a striptease of zealous mantras. The Allah worshiper's rear is high in the air, the sadhu's head deep in a bucket of sand. A scribe fills his gold-tip pen and scribbles insincere fakeries for anxious illiterates who extend blue paper rupees.

Diversions, consequences. Semblances, divinations . . .

The multitude contracts and expands—an anemone, a pointellist painting spilling boundaries, dots of color exchanging places. A traveler bunks with the devil of confusion and confronts the victory of illusion, hoping to clarify the nature and limits of the self. The tourist can't take it. He wishes to reduce pandemonium to reason and satisfy the mind. He opts to hold a camera between city and eye. But when a fakir with a saw blade through his chest stumbles up and claws at him for a coin, it's back to the air-conditioned hotel—thank you—for sweetened tea and an eclair. Life is so close to death here that one cannot participate in the city without realizing that flesh begins from absences. And into absence returns. With a disarranged twinkle, Varanasi teases the mind:

"Why do we buy things in life, why do we try to get anywhere?"

We invent the hand of God to guide us through our own dilemma. Families, cities, nations dissolve and reconjugate like corpuscles in the bloodstream. Heads bang with noise and misfortune. Jets roar above superimposed dialects and bell gong. Bank notes are traded upstairs, while in the gutter vendors pump their cheeks, shriek poetic lines over pointed falsies whose maroon tips bleed in the sun. One guy calculates profit above used hair nets and miniature Elvises in heart-shaped bottles that snow when you turn them upside down. Another entertains potential buyers as he flips through bright calendars of Iranian princesses boarding fighter planes, Kali drinking blood from entwined lovers, a Bombay movie star halting a tank with his bare hand.

Before dawn all was silent under the cold stars. The vendors were not in place. An ethereal blue filled the east. The city grew light with prayer and chanting. Priests sat at the shore with flames in their hands. Women were busy with their purchases of flower petals, scented oils and milk to anoint the holy phalluses set inside white marble yonis facing the Ganges.

81

Within minutes, though, Varanasi stretched, yawned, rubbed soot from its eyes and realized it was alive after another hard night. Then. . . all hell broke loose.

Money changers set up their abacus racks. Prayer turned to hawkers' cries. Body fought body in mad scramble to bathe at the ghats; or toward gushing faucets for rituals of teeth scrubbing and repugnant gargles. To the thump of mattress pounding, men and women began a serious contest of hacks and coughs brought about by fingers down throats. In one short breath, dawn become loud, obscene, angry; like sugared rice pudding softened on the tongue, then suddenly acrid with a rancidness come about after centuries of fermentation. The sky closed like a red-rimmed eye. The mob brought up mad choruses of incantations mixed with toxic coughs of phlegm scoured from the lungs:

UUUUUUUUUUUUuuuuwwwwwww   *hhheeeehaw*
UUUUUuuuuuu   *Sssssoooooowwwwf!*   *eh   eh   ehhhhh ewwwwk!*
hatha hew hew hew   *hatha hew hew hew*   .   .   .

I stood in the crow's nest, ears filling with oblique howls, brash rumblings, weird play of opposites. I allowed them in, strangely unrepulsed by it all: the prayer, grim defecations, loose bowels of chatter, coins spilling, the *jai jai ram* of a funeral procession blending with the noisy Rosicrucian scrubbing his vegetarian pans next door.

Earthquakes, silences, cacophony . . .

Amid the rowdiness and bangs, the crescendos and diminuendos, I realized not only soot and dust were being vomited from those poor citizens' lungs, but that a strange exorcism was in process—the

82

purposeful ridding of whatever evil had entered their dreams by night to make the body unclean by day.

※

What should I ask for this morning?

A geyser, an ice floe, a penetrating star, a bouquet of nerves to meter the smoke screens, a Buddha tongue to taste every incomprehensible stopping place I will move through during the day? Like it or not, I am set to sail. The world is a drug, a sea, a noxious eyelash winking out lifetimes which we expect to last. But there is only momentary balance in the crosscurrents of a great circle that won't close. Or perhaps not a circle at all, but an unending spiral consuming itself as it narrows inward.

The journey—with its emotions and revelations, confused tributaries and wayward players, perfumed valleys and nocturnal jungles—is not for escape nor for entertainment. It is a motion entirely of its own, a curious vigil within the dream, an open eye of departures and dizzy arrivings where I awaken to another's existence—and to another me. Great travail, numerous difficulties: they are there to test, to see if I am strong enough to walk with resilience, to live profoundly each new day.

Go to a faraway land and travel becomes all about finding a new way home. Unplugged from my usual reality, the particulars of others' lives flood in. But there is a paradox. As a traveler I am moved by people who stay in place. Without them, what questions, revelations, affirmations? My insights are inspired largely by destitute people bound to households, caged by culture, enslaved by caste. They cannot move. I can. They're too poor to afford medicine. My bag is filled with prescriptions. They wallow in the Bangladesh cyclone. I escape the debris by rail or stay for awhile and begin to feel part of "my" new home. But I am aloof, a visitor from another planet inspecting, dissecting, reporting on others' lives. At any given moment—when the going gets rough, when the sun edges into eclipse or the dictator pulls his trigger—I can grab the next flight out.

More than any other moment in history, time and space have been shrunk. But despite this enormous shrinking of distance, the accessibility of distant places doesn't mean that travelers having means to visit them will do so with inspiration or insight. In this age of the global village, place has become a commodity. Once-remote Shangrilas, vine-tangled Angkor Watts, the secret puberty rites of tribal peoples, all the pagodas, Forbidden Cities, mythic peaks, tombs, Grand Canyons, erotic megaliths, sacred ventholes and hidden villages of wise old *curanderos* can now be "had" via new-age travel bureaus. Cultural tours, vision quests, shamanic journeys, eco tours, medicine tours, even "healing" tours have been packaged to fit busy people questing an experience outside themselves to fulfill an inner investigation they've never allowed.

A young backpacker from Chile, traveling with his Japanese girlfriend, recited a grand list of continents "covered" in nine months of journey, but in the same breath admitted that they were taking a long break in order to investigate *how* they had been *where* they traveled. I liked that confrontation. And the hard fact of his realization that "culture too, another commodity." Traditional peoples must now serve strangers, leave their crops, make public private ceremonies, learn the lingua franca of the world, and of marketeers.

In our eager quest to disengage from the stress of self-imposed routines, we have intruded on others' daily cycles, diminishing their values by lugging along our own. Soon, what we came for will be gone, what we yearned to be rid of will greet us ever-more-consistently when we arrive. The Sufi thinker Indries Shah observed: "a tourist is one who goes to a place which was originally worth visiting. He is undoubtedly endowed with supernatural powers, because after sufficient exposure to the tourist, the inhabitants start to hate the place."

※

The big clock on Dasaswamedh Lane gongs noon.

I open the door and stroll into the blazon images seen from above. The crowd explodes like a supernova. Greasy foreheads pasted with third eyes. A goddess whose cleavage drips hot wax. Mumbling defecators below a painted acrobat bending backwards inside a fiery hoop to announce: **THE NEW VARANASI CIRCUS.** For years my pen will work to decipher the standstill wreck of this adventure. Right now I wonder why we are all so quiet as we shout each other out of the way. Who knows who in this potpourri? The pundit is too busy talking to know his congregation. The beggar too busy asking to know his almsgiver. Even the most intimate lovers dwell in shadow play.

Up close the city clock is faceless. What striking announced high noon? Perhaps it was the tomfoolery of a monkey reaching inside the clock's belly to knock its pendulum—an act probably sanctioned by city officials in response to years under British schedules. At the clock's base, two mutts locked in intercourse whine as they struggle to uncopulate. At my feet, a powder puff lands from an open window as a blind man knocks his stick against me.

✖

Mandanpura Road.

Another busy market place. A faded daguerreotype pock marked at center, blurred at the edges. Spirit walkers shuffling in dreamplay. Peeling facades, abandoned mike stands, sidewalk card players puffing water pipes. Bananas frying in one vat, a bucket of tar boiling in another—both over the same fire. Up to the hearth walks a young ragamuffin, a charcoal vendor with a burlap bag over her smeared shoulder, a jasmine flower wilting in her hair. She could be twelve years old. Or nineteen. She could be a key half-turned inside a lock to a sleeping passageway.

"I be your guide?"

✖

First to a decrepit shrine, where an ascetic wearing an orange breechcloth prays before a broken statue of Hanuman. From a distance he is tanned and graceful, mixing yogic poses with a ballet of tantric Tai Chi. Up close he reveals a frighteningly burned face. I want to turn away, yet part of me remains transfixed by his scarred and repaired flesh—skin taught and shiny like that of a bat in broad daylight.

Suddenly he turns and sticks out a tongue pierced with a gold ring dangling with an amber bead. It looks like a salamander's eye. I turn away, then stand blinking at the crumbling statue of Hanuman, its head knocked off centuries ago by invading Muslims. The ascetic seems perfectly content to pray before this half-crumbled, decapitated statue. Instead of Hanuman's head, he honors a blazing bougainvillea erupting from the broken neck.

"Your name?" I ask the girl.
"Amarjeet" she replies, continuing her brisk pace.

Her hair is a nest of henna-colored Dravidian locks falling upon sun-blackened shoulders. She is frail, already bent from man-size loads of charcoal. Yet there is something about her sway, the generous mouth, the sturdy curve of the neck, the ravishing glance of her eye that calls forth the woman in her, a figure from an ancient frieze who struggles to unscramble a line of Hindi into English:

"My wanting to take you to Shiva tree."

And we regain momentum. Into a narrow street jammed with men loitering on steps, holding hands, adjusting penises, fingering nostrils, going at the spaces between toes. Farmers gulping mouth-ringed dirty glasses of lukewarm tea. Merchants guarding change boxes. Curers sorting degutted hummingbirds. A get-rich-quick kid arranging "Special Import Sexaphones" and blackened bottles of "My Sore Catsup."

Men, everywhere, their incessant talk an off-tune orchestra of riddles and preoccupied syllables. Men, whose parrot mouths rattle like abacuses above faded lingerie, "Butler Automatic Toilet Paper," garlic oil and bags of powdered antler. Men, busy making themselves visible, while women make themselves invisible—behind walls, inside tents, in barbed-wire compounds, wrapped in nine meters of silk, moving under black cotton canopies, eying the world through gauze peepholes—as proscribed. Women, and the daughters of women, under tubs of human excrement, baskets of dirty laundry, loads of dough. Laying roads. Cracking stone.

Hammering granite into gravel at the construction site of the new Grand Empress Hotel. Tent rows of them: feeding fires, nursing babies, slapping chapatis, skinning bone, hauling milk, mending wounds, pounding stone.

And this dirtied slave to the charcoal trade?

Married in a few years? Bearing children as a young teen? Chained by the groom's family, kept from school, sent to clean latrines, threatened with matches if she doesn't bear a son? Laboring, laboring. To help her husband ahead in a society designed only for his benefit?

※

Varanasi, it does not quit. Night and day, an unhalting roulette wheel of voluptuous buttocks under perfumed silk, festering arm stumps poking from rags. Blocks of dry ice under hissing blow torches. Scaffolds of wealth. Terrible youth in yellow shade. Hard fists. Cataract eyes. A man wrapped inside a nest of cobras. A woman selling prohibited meat. The heat of puberty. The crooked jaw of death. The world invents itself as I watch. Hundreds of movie projectors collapse in a heap, each projecting a different reel on the same screen. The world is an apparition we try to complete. Perpetual multiplicities seen through an eye wrenched from the body, splintered into mirrors, struggling to make sense in a sea of heads burlesquing with nos that are meant to say yes.

The Shiva tree is in the heart of the Panchaganga neighborhood, where five rivers mysteriously converge underground. "One of many such Shiva shrines in India," the Brahmin caretaker exclaims. "But this one is best. Es-pec-ially sacred. Look here, see . ."

Inside a hollow in the trunk, blue flames wreathe a glistening marble lingam. The Brahmin asks for money. My little guide waves me away. Angered, the priest hides his tray of garlands and refuses his blessing. As we exit the park she points to a propane tank behind the shrine hooked to a copper line that feeds the miraculous flame.

Toward the Ganges—across the cracked sidewalk in front of Hotel Runs where medicine men peddle sleeping tablets and bootleg diarrhea pills—is a traffic zone of human wheelbarrows. Puffing, sweating Dickens-like characters grimacing under loads of commerce: sewing machines, bananas, newspaper, gasoline, mangos. Impossible bundles of greasy rags, the men beneath them absolutely indistinguishable from the loads they carry. One porter plods toward a music shop, nearly collapsing under the huge plaster dog he is carrying, a dog printed with the slogan: "His Master's Voice."

The day is straight up. Nothing has a shadow. We enter unrecognizable gullis devoted to death: henna for corpse feet, scented powders for pyres, sweet grass and ghee to ignite fires, a thousand meters of corpse cloth, a hundred tubs of white chrysanthemums, printed mantras, recorded wails, calligraphed prayer books, plastic ash containers, cloves to relieve the mind, incense for the nasal cavity.

At the river's edge is an imposing figure carved from an enormous chunk of basalt. Not a he, not a she—but a towering hermaphrodite blackened with oil, smeared with vermilion powder, pasted with dried flowers. A great knot of hair above a seductive face. Sleek and pointed Aryan nose. Big Buddha ears. Eyes and lips protruding with an enigmatic "Yes." One side of the chest is sculpted into a woman's breast, the other built like a weight lifter's. The pelvis is half male, half female, symmetrically balanced above one leg thick like a warrior's, the other fluidly curved like a classical court dancer's.

Statue blinks. Beholders blink . .

A dark yet radiant metaphor for wholeness here. My guide is neither embarrassed nor restrained, but at ease in front of this deity whose mythology has been part of her world since birth.

"Who is this?"

"Shiva Half Female," she says.

A he, a she—the twofold nature of ourselves, of the universe, singularized into one paradoxical, benevolent being. I look down. Amarjeet looks up. She is about to go. I hear her wings begin to blaze, see the little body scatter a glow from within its Dravidian darkness. Then I catch my mind calculating, totally removed from the magic of this afternoon, the initiation this girl has given me. She will certainly want a *baksheesh*; I'll certainly pay her more than enough. A ridiculous amount — spoiling things for travelers to come. But I am about to do it. Her hand is moving upwards. Her eyes . . and then she breaks away, looks to the water, bows to the river . . and returns a smoldering gaze. Six little words fill the air, not from her mouth, but suspended around her body:

"I liking you. You liking me?"

Off she scampers. She does not wait for money. She does not look back. An inaudible call? Something, someone, pulling her like a magnet? Yet who, or from where, I know not. But a luminous presence lingers. That of someone who's seen this world before. And come again to give it greater meaning.

✖

It is late. Paraffin candles cast soft light from their cellophane shrouds. The night market glows like a ragged altar. Tables are covered with candies and sweetmeats bagged in recycled textbook pages printed with mathetmatical equations. Peanut vendors have replaced daytime hawkers. The homeless are here too—bundled in dirty cloth on the sidewalk, exchanging muffled good nights as moviegoers step over them. At my apartment door there is an itinerant magician performing with his son. A circle of spectators is gathered by lantern light. The magician orders the boy beneath a sequined cloth, brandishes a cudgel and slams it upon him.

A sickening *thummmmmp!*
A gasp . .

The boy's head has been lopped off. With his foot, the magician rolls it apart from the body under the cloth. He says that for ten rupees he'll replace the head. A donation appears. The magician chants a spell. Snaps away the colored cloth. The boy stands up in perfect condition. A round of applause. Spectators disperse.

Once, near this same doorway at a tiny wooden table at a tea stall, I pondered the inevitable question of why I had come to India. Wrapped in soliloquy, I did not bother to acknowledge the tea man as he set down a glass of hot *chai*. Obsessed with maintaining my thoughts, I fumbled for change and paid him without looking up. But the man remained, his stained apron visible from the periphery of my eye. Finally, I looked at

91

him. He was standing like an idol, holding a tray of empty glasses—smoking a cigarette through a hole in his forehead, puffing smoke rings through his teeth!

"A terrible misfortune" he explained. "I was shot by a thief attempting a train robbery near Allahabad. By the will of the Divine Guru I recovered—but with this awful wound. I have made the best of it though. I use my ugliness to attract business, to amuse customers like you."

At that moment my question was answered. I had come to India because here it is possible to find in reality what one sees only in dreams. A cigarette is inhaled through the forehead, not the mouth. The guardian of the Ganges is neither a strong man in classic proportions nor a graceful goddess, but a towering fusion of both. A magician and son appear in front of a dark but familiar doorway not by coincidence, but as meditative symbols telling me I am here to have my head chopped off, my mind severed from its usual perspective of self.

A doorway opens. Myth and reality merge in overwhelming proportions. From the balcony spreads a renamed world. India is the antithesis of the walled garden created by my parents to protect their idea of how I should live, who I should grow up to be. Here, more than any other place in the world, is a land where opposites are magnified and life is larger than itself. "Lucid unreason," Artaud wrote. "This is all one can say. It is the logic of Illogic."

※

Sunrise, Varanasi.

It always comes back to this. The yellow disk going white. The great Hindu Eucharist self elevating without reflection in the river over which it rises. Solar wafer. Surya of blinding energy. Medusa of tangled rays warping the angled skies, drawing water from root to branch, allowing taste to fill the buds, and questions—questions!—to landslide between the fingers. Dust, locomotive smoke, green stations inside the bride's gown, tide of unstopping persuasions mooring themselves to the body like tea leaves in portentous configurations at the bottom of a cup. To walk these streets is to walk disrobed, an apparition inside someone else's interrogation. Yesterday hasn't happened. The future is past. Every question in India raises a double edge, one applicable to personal life, it's existential chronology; the other to a subconscious realm where time spirals from archetypal past to mythic present.

One boards a train, travels horizontally over a parched plain, enters a thunderhead, succumbs to the alchemy of the monsoon. The mind tumbles into a vertical world of self examination, dry dust, catatonic haze, wet texture, muddy complexity. Train wheels grind. Hot metal fills the throat. For every hitchhiker along the way—farmer with hen, grandmother plastered with medicinal leaves, vendor lugging in suitcase—the train halts. In a wreathe of greasy steam the conductor waves a ragged flag.

Four men are at the tracks. Robbers disguised as farm hands? Countrymen looking like thugs? Neither. As soon as they lift a bier from the bushes and begin to board the train it is clear that they are members of a funeral party. The conductor hurries to bar them from boarding with the corpse. The engineer looks back and throttles his machine. Crows scatter, black smoke boils over the parched landscape. The chase is on. The corpse head—wrapped like a mummy—jiggles back and forth on its bamboo bier. The funeral party runs alongside the rattling carriages, almost dumping the corpse in its mad pursuit. But the train is too fast. They slip from view into the dusty briar. Steam blurs the dead fields. Sun boils and spins an unbreathable cloud of dust through dry riverbeds.

My mind flickers off like a lamp. Retina is an empty shell. I open my travel bag, look into a mirror—but no reflection returns. Instead, there is a bride stripped bare in the glass. Her anguish is that of the wedding night—emotional death in the darkness of a foreign land; the ambiguity of an unfamiliar chamber where a complete stranger now invades her most private parts. Then to sleep, to drift, to wake in the aftermath—like Lazarus walking into the sun, filled with new life.

※

Varanasi—you grow cloudy.
Where have I been?
Who stepped out to walk with me?
How long have I slept, or have I slept at all?
Is day is about to break or has dusk fallen?

The gods play tricks from their alcoves. Vishnu floats on his back in a bath of drowned clocks. Parvati milks each breast to clear the poison from her body. The city is an eye with a hook in its center. Only my heart knows the truth of the details. That by day I strolled through shadows, watched streets fill, stared into misery, madness, pools of youth, skies flapping with vultures indistinguishable from children's kites. That by night, when my shadow slipped over the gutter's purple rim where the beggars found rest—someone else joined me. Our boatman struggled upstream against the Ganges, his oars splitting the moon into shards as distant pyres wheeled their sparks into the opposite flow of the Milky Way. And afterwards, with transfigured darkness surrounding, she returned up the stairs with me, stood on the balcony, called it 'a starblown deck of a vagrant ship', then turned and took me, saying "No, don't bathe. Let's be together with the smoke of the dead."

So many impressions here—submerged, evaporated . . .

The mind asks for more details, but receives only a mirage. I close my book on the balcony, but my handwriting continues its weave, dangling from the page like a spider's filament. dropping through memory, jilted skylines, fractured chasms of quartz and steel. A storm breaks. A voice calls from the hallway. Deserts erupt from the sea. Rain ices into snowlines. The street empties its multitude into shadows. I hear names of other people. See phantoms trumpeting from color, shapes released from destiny. I look carefully into each palm.

Empty . . .

In the revelation of the world, I have been taken from myself. Where did I begin before me? How is it I walk through a room of darkness that is all windows? That there is no sound yet someone stares back? That light is released when the hands move? Varanasi, your eye fits in mine. Elusive fathom, dark star, gold upon green magnetized in dawn's melancholy. Today I will rise and walk and walk and walk until the horizon is clear. I will fill my teeth with dust, plant a seed, keep my promises.

I will seek the dream that sounds my name.

▓

जय माता दी तेरे सेवक रहे पुकार बोलो जय माता दी

आरती श्री अम्बाजी की

DURGA PUJA AT THE GANGES

Durga's day is in November, when the moon is right and the constellations auspiciously placed. At twilight, on the very spot where Vishnu stepped from heaven, Durga—the fierce aspect of the All Mother Goddess—is paraded. She is clay-daubed, fashioned from papier maché, adorned with plastic jewels. Each of her hands brandishes a warrior's emblem: trident, discus, thunder-bolt, conch shell, club, bouquet of snakes. Her teeth are bared, her ten arms whirl over trays of sweets, heaps of flowers and clay bowls of curd.

Durga is Shiva's counterpart. The personification of female energy. A fertility divinity. Destroyer. Cleanser. Axe grinder. Venerated slayer of mind demons. Her burning eyes shift menacingly. Her huge buttocks spread around the giant tiger she rides. Her arms reach over the universe. Her enormous breasts spin like wheels above exaggerated hips pasted with sandalwood and basil leaves. On wooden beams, high above the masses, she is raised. To the off-melody scream of horns and jazz-thump of drums she is paraded to the river—and ceremoniously dumped. Half submerged, her tempera make up, her gold foil, her jeweled third eye, her necklace of seeds, her cardboard weapons melt in the churning flow.

Downstream she drifts, carried by Himalayan meltwater to the Bay of Bengal. As she disintegrates to a litany of *Oms*, her shiny cloth unravels. A priest raises his smoking censer over what is left of her body. Bells clang, pelvises move. The heated multitude sways nervously. Intense perspiration soaks women's saris. Glazed eyeballs roll inside men's fiery sockets. The river ghats crack and collapse with devotees seeking

97

darshan—presence—of the All Mother Goddess.

Children, parents, beggars, queens, policemen, prostitutes, musicians, monkeys, the prime minister: all bend to the water and pray. Some release miniature leaf rafts pinned together with toothpicks, filled with flower petals and candles. At twilight the fever heightens. The river dances with stars. The air quakes with miasmic fusion of bells, chanting throats, censer smoke and earth-painted bodies.

Durga's day in India. At the most sacred of all pilgrimage spots of the Ganges. A vortex of whirlpools and exaggerated cloud formations assure that this place is indeed a *tirtha,* an intersection between earth and heaven. Today, no need to "believe"—only to arrive, to name, to chant, to be present and thus automatically be redeemed from countless future rebirths, hundreds of past evils.

※

Through the frenzy of bleating horns and chattering Oms, runaway cows and seething bodies in polychrome sway, I sense a time when devotion was more austere, the religious overlay lacking, a largely-animist indigenous population absorbed in a quiet worship. Paying tribute to sacred groves. Planting terra-cotta figurines between banyan roots. Honoring source waters bubbling from springs. Admiring magic chameleons changing color upside down on branches. Listening to amphibious beings announce the monsoon rains. Honoring beautifully-swaying snakes, their shapes and movement symbolic of male reproductivity.

Then, the Aryans arrived following the Ganges into Dravidian India, fusing animist water worship with their gods of fire and sun. Soon, the birth of prayer, caste, taxes—the highly organized Hindu religion. Brahma, Vishnu and Shiva with their various consorts and manifestations, forming a sacred triad above an elaborate pantheon that would be endlessly expanded over the millennia. At some point Durga would be born. From her old home in village caves, she would eventually find place in temples, solidify into plastic, appear on metal refrigerator magnets, and explode her third-eye ray from lithographed wall calendars.

Wild tribesmen honor with many a victim
Durga, goddess of the Forest who dwells in rocks and caves,
pouring blood to the local Genius at the tree.
Then, joined by their women at day's end, they alternate
the gourd lyre's merriment with rounds of liquor
drunk from bilva cups.

This Durga rite was described by Yogesvara, an 8th-century Sanskrit poet. Today, the identical rite continues, but the old blood sacrifice meant to appease Durga's thirstiness—or simply to return life force back into the body of the earth—has been replaced by splashing red dye and colored water into the faces of icons and devotees. North of the Ganges, in Kathmandu, however, Durga's thirst *is* quenched with blood. During the autumn festival of Dasain, hundreds of goats and water buffalo are slaughtered before her effigy.

Durga is a demanding goddess. She must not only be honored communally, but privately. Homes must be sprinkled with water, swept, surrounded with marigolds. Fields should receive plantings of grain. Roses must be purchased. Jasmine and champa blossoms are essential. Hearths need to be impeccably cleaned. Durga's icon asks for splashes of perfume and precious oils. Her long hair must be combed and braided into wild rivulets falling down her back. Braids like the monsoon rain surging from Himalayan slopes to nourish India's dry plain.

"Durga's eyes are crossed. She sees both ways at once," a young sales woman in a tourist emporium explains. The sales woman herself is an aspect of Durga. A youthful tree dressed in green silk printed with leaf designs. Her thinly-sandaled feet are the color of the clay floor beneath her. Through a back door into a courtyard I see her children—two girls—perform the ancient ritual of bringing trees to fruition by kicking them gently with bare feet while a hired musician plays his wooden flute. A holdover from how many hundreds of centuries past?

"Puja" means worship. Today Durga is the recipient of this worship. As she dissolves in the Ganges, worshipers' prayers journey with her to the sea, evaporate into the universe. Thin hands join in supplication. Durga submerges, then bobs suddenly to surface, returning crosseyed glances into the soul of humanity. She looks at the living and reminds us of the dead. She sees drought in one eye, cyclones in the other. She ponders mortality, smiles at eternity. She frees us from malice, burns away greed.

▓

THE SOURCE OF THE PERSONIFICATION OF SHIVA

The mountains work on the psyche of the people. They are there in the eye. They penetrate the unconscious. They lift their folded wings into the sun's mouth, into the moon's silver cruet. They begin deep beneath the horizon and end just before the stars. The mountains float between children's swings, between the wooden rungs of village Ferris wheels. They spread icy wings over timber-stripped folds, over pastures and footpaths, frangipani and whitewashed shrines. Over birch, oak, fir, deodar and rhododendron they choreograph storms. The mountains are makers of clouds, guardians of springs. They begin the day and make rivers flow. Their canyons hide yetis and snow leopards.

Mendicants perch before turquoise cascades, reciting mantras, performing yoga, clicking prayer beads while ice whiskers form on their legs and chests. Pilgrims ascend the ice floes, half naked, flagging innumerable shrines. Traders herd yaks, porters lug merchandise to the feet of bosses who dwell far behind the mountains, in the shadows of their peaks.

In Europe or North America one may experience the psychological change, the change in spirit that mountains bring. But nowhere on the planet is this change more powerful than when a traveler begins on the immense Indian plateau and works upward to the Himalayan wall; works through stifling cities and parched multitudes, the choking plains whose blistered edges curl like onionskin into the ruthless horizon.

From thousands of miles south the pilgrims come. Bending in full body prostrations, meter by meter, kilometer by kilometer, until the first sight of Langtang or Dorje-Lakpa, framed with poinsettia flowers, brightens the eye. The Himalayan wall rises like a ladder into the clouds, mixing mists with snow banners and snow banners with jet-stream cirrus. The sight immediately reminds the pilgrim that ours is an imperfect copy of another world. A world higher up from the the flatlands of everyday activities.

Architects of stupas, pagodas, ziggurats, cathedrals—as well as the builders of Macchu Picchu or the sky villages of the American Southwest—understood the allegorical aspects of geography; its metaphor; the primal need to "go up." They matched their architectural skills with internal quests and stepped closer to heaven. To where sunlight and rain are born. To where the air is thin, the light rare, the atmosphere needled with vibrations unencountered below.

All architecture of the sacred resembles the mountain. The ziggurat spirals upward like smoke into the stars, each tier representing a celestial cycle, a spiritual plateau. The stupa rearranges the Elemental Peak into abstract three-dimensional mandalas piled one on top of the other to represent earth, water, fire, air, ether. The pagoda hangs gracefully in mid air like a bell, a mountain flower. The pyramid represents perpetuity, eternity, the beauty of precision, the mystery of equations. The Gothic window shines gloriously into a sanctuary of prayer, its rarefied wavelengths counterfeiting high-altitude light, the glacial translucence of solitary ice fields near Ama Dablam's summit, or the throne of Chomolungma whose ice-chiseled face spreads a pinkened aura across Khumbu Glacier. The sculptured lingam, so important to Hindu ritual, replicates the lone pinnacle that penetrates heaven's blue. A reverse cosmology is implied: earth is male; its warm pinnacle thrusts into the female body of sky which is cool, all surrounding. Condensation takes place. A storm is born.

Shiva's power came from the mountains. On Kailash he meditated, gained sight. Today, as in past generations, pilgrims trek through rain forests and ice crags to reach the Tibetan plateau from which pokes the earth's central axis: Mt. Kailash. Once there, the presence of the mountain is enough. No need to conquer it. Instead, the pilgrim hunkers down to boil a pot of tea then packs bedroll on shoulder and sets out to circumnavigate the mountain. The trek is as much metaphysical as it is physical. Rounding Kailash, the pilgrim realizes that the mountain is a snow-covered lingam, the source of the personification of Shiva.

And what of times before the Hindus, when the mountain had yet to be abstracted into the lingam? Rudra, the Howler, the Lightning-spitting One, was Shiva's Vedic predecessor. Pelting the lowlands with rain and hail, Rudra—whose origins reach into the Paleolithic—was the terrifying deity of high mountains. The White-faced One who could unpredictably turn dark with tempest, brighten with fire. Rudra: the pre-Aryan roarer whose voice was associated with the bull, symbol of virility and fertility basic to hunting and planting cults alike.

Shiva, then, as Rudra.
Shiva, with his phallic-humped bull, Nandi.

Shiva, colored blue with wood ash. The blue of fire's aftermath. The blue of rarefied atmosphere, the metaphysical ocean upon which all thoughts, all continents float. The blue of unaltered pure-stream consciousness. This is the Shiva who the modern sadhu imitates, personifies, venerates. The Shiva who, with lightning wand and cosmic drum, sits perfectly erect over the world in trance meditation, voice thundering powerfully through valleys of mist and terraced grain. It is Shiva's dance that turns the cosmos. A dance of birth, death, regeneration. A dance of volcanic eruption. Glaciers grinding continents. The torrential flood that submerges Bangladesh. The tsunami of the Pacific. The tsunami of the mind.

All across the Indian subcontinent Shiva is worshiped. His caste-bronze idol is showered with marigolds. His hair reels outward like sun spokes, fertility snakes, jets of water exploding from a thunderhead. His dance of destruction and rebirth is painted on scrolls, carried through cities, pasted on rickshaw buggies, displayed on army jeeps, smuggled into antique shops, glued to restaurant walls, made into pastries, earrings and automobile decals. His infinite store of reproductive power is replicated in metal, ivory, jade, alabaster, granite, plastic, tourmaline and glass. Smooth, hard, eternally erect, splashed with coconut milk, oiled with camphor, greased with body sweat, sat on in Tantric rituals, circled with live snakes, smeared with ashes of the dead, his stone lingam is the mystical reproductive symbol of India.

But Shiva's real praise is given unconsciously everywhere in India and Nepal as people go about their daily tasks. When the Pokhara knife grinder spins his stone and sparks fly, Shiva dances. When the children of Dhulikel chant rhyme songs from the seats of their wooden Ferris wheels, Shiva dances. When the butter maid in Ahmadabad churns her milk, when oxen wheels squeak under massive loads of peas and lentils en route to Kanpur, when mischievous monkeys spin the Swayambhunath prayer wheels, when bright-aproned women thresh wheat in circular movements or switch open the water gates to power their mill wheels—they become participants in Shiva's primal dance.

Nowhere but within sight of the planet's highest mountains is this cosmic aspect of the universe—the galactic spin of all living things, the mundane yet sacred rotation of one human around another, of moon around earth and earth around sun—more emphasized. The fulcrum-working peasants lifting water from one canal to another in rhythmic dance, the snow banners spiraling from the summits of Machhapuchhare, the eery pyre smoke coiling from the ghats at Pashupatinath, or an infant twisting its newly-grown locks with a tiny set of fingers: these are the many arms of the Eternal Dancer who creates and destroys our universe daily; who floods our senses with light and shadow. This is Shiva, whose circular steps keep the world round, whose cosmic song puts the universe in perpetual motion.

※

KATHMANDU, A CANTO

Without notion of direction my feet place themselves one in front of the other, side stepping androgynous deities, hopping obstructions, falling upon incomprehensible surfaces. Languages clutter and separate in the ear. Tourists blur inside the eye as they flee fossil vendors and money changers, or move hurriedly toward raucous parades of fanatic Hindus tooting horns behind celibate butts of horse-drawn goddesses. Clouds loosen from snow peaks, anchor themselves to pagoda tops. But the city goes about its business in dust.

All afternoon it has been wanting to rain. Despite the clanging bells, the offerings of fire and the chanting monks, no moisture falls. Behind the painted wheel of liberation a monkey smiles. A fat sow rubs her snout against the decaying boundaries of her pen. Lard boils in the sun. A lotus wilts on Parvati's throne. I aim for the mosquito on my arm, slap myself instead. The world is occult, filled with prophesy, pathos, an air of pulverized light.

In the butcher district an eyeball stares from the sidewalk. Meat cutters sleep on mattresses wedged inside half-slaughtered carcasses. Lanterns, knives, towels, mirrors, framed cinema goddesses hang from cows' ribs. Clear plastic bags are filled with shining intestines and miscellaneous hooves oozing jelly. Mama's Pie Shop, next to Third Eye Travels, is splattered with blood from last week's festival. A sign in Tit Bits Tea Parlour reads: "Fresh Milk Lassies."

One sees the ochre villages and checkered fields from the air, descends

109

into a jeweled green landscape from the clouds, and expects an impeccable fairyland of clean-swept cobble, beauty without meanness, the purity of snow and fresh air, rose gardens and merciful icons. But it ends at the airport, right after the customs inspector rummages through your belongings and, either by mistake or as a deliberate joke, stamps your hand instead of the passport.

The taxi man crams seven of you from every part of the world, each speaking a different language and holding a different political card, into a midget automobile, and off you go smoking down the pot-holed tarmac toward the inner city. Immediately the fairyland breaks down. The taxi pulls to a stoplight behind a cartload of bleeding goat heads. An old baba, with a head like a water pump and a face of twisted leather, walks along fanning incense on live coals in a cavity of his slumped chest. Through emblematic trash heaps in dead-end alleys, a dwarf picks her way.

Everything is static, in electric standstill. As if the movie reel had snapped. As if a roofless cathedral had suddenly collapsed on a congregation waiting for the moon to catch up with the sun or mill wheels to synchronize with astrological predictions. A breeze blows but the banner strung between police station and public library does not move:

SPEAK THE TRUTH PERFORM YOUR DHARMA
DO NOT FAIL FROM SELF STUDY

A child in bright pink underpants plays hopscotch, blowing a Nepalese pop tune through a leaf between her lips. My hand circumscribes the clouds, the old baba, the child, the smoldering trash heaps, and ends on the chin of this strange human animal who embraces mediocrities, feels emotion, watches the world dissolve and recompose.

110

In every direction the city leaps its skin, devours hills, coughs a yellow smog line before the dreamy Himalayan peaks. Bamboo scaffolding, cement buckets lashed with rope, fresh planks cut and spliced into the geometry of human need. Impossible not to feel every inert beam and post as once breathing entities waving their branches in the sun. Brick houses, brick courtyards, brick temples, brick offices. Bricks heaped in sagging dump trucks, bricks on backs of women. Bricks piled under the bat-infested trees surrounding the King's palace. How many trees to fire one kiln load of brick?

Who was it that asked:

"If the world is so beautiful, why are we not beautiful in it?"

Vishnu's bell is cracked by an earthquake. The Fire Goddess happily guards her intimate curves. The Muslim mango man climbs toward heaven on a sword. The Hindu saint undresses a thin-bloused punk rocker with his all-seeing third eye. Black market gem cutters cultivate plastic where there should be sapphire. Tanners screw their noses over putrid hides. The balls of a gentle beast are castrated under a transistor radio playing the national anthem while an air force of flies prepares its attack.

The daydream is mortal. Our identities temporal, interchangeable. My eyes follow shifting moments, discover a metaphor in the child's kite soaring upward so fast as to become invisible, then taking an unexpected nosedive into a high-tension line new to the city's outskirts. The afternoon crinkles like cellophane. Tailors whir their bobbins, embroider while-you-wait Om signs. Clouds build in front of dreamy peaks, then part to reveal the same summits metamorphosized into jagged fangs ready to devour the world of human hustle and startling taboos. We, who maneuver to the best seat, the quickest nirvana, the highest profit, the perfect island.

Over there is a guy refusing to be himself. He wears highbeam cufflinks to a political rally in a hotel full of broken tables. One block away, Kali sleeps under a stone bridge in headgear of old sweaters, her spindly legs ending in broken flipflops. High above, the King and Queen's cutout cardboard portrait is displayed for easy veneration while they tour Copenhagen, squandering the country's tax money on a shopping spree.

※

A sign points to the Temple of the Living Goddess. A child of premenstrual age with khol-darkened eyes and crystal crown who, I am told, might be possible to see. But when ushered into the dilapidated courtyard below her half-curtained window, I find that only for a hefty baksheesh will she appear. Better, and for free, are the erotic maidens celebrating the eternal play of procreation carved high on roof supports over the city's open-air shrines. One lies on her stomach, suckles her child and raises her buttocks to a winged partner who penetrates her from behind. Another reclines on her back, presses her breasts together and spreads her legs with delight to the erect head of a flower. Another copulates with her lover while riding a horse who simultaneously copulates with another horse.

Across the rickety bridge over the Vishnumati River, the city ends. Hills and fields begin. Crickets chant acoustical signals in terraced mustard greens. A cement mixer burps as its motor turns. A house is being constructed from the materials of another being torn down. A family is

112

spread between them both—lighting hearth fires in one, going to bed in the other.

A footpath zigzags like a slow fuse through cabbage plots and poinsettias toward the thick woods of Swayambhunath Hill, its top crowned by a huge stupa whose gold tower is painted with Buddha's omnipresent eyes. Festive yet imposing, they scan crops, overlook human activities, keep track of kingfishers, make sure the cows are fed. Over births, weddings, deaths, funerals and every connected ritual, they preside. Staring upward at the great stupa, I see a spiral of calligraphy under those powerful eyes. Calligraphy that to the Nepalese means "One" but to the westerner looks like an upside down question mark. An appropriate symbol, in a land where euphoria and the grotesque are inseparable.

Between rich homes and poor, stone walls and bamboo, the trail weaves. Upon it my shadow is an enigma, a figure swaying in and out of itself, always arriving, never quite formed. A hologram whose recombining energies form ungraspable edges.

※

All is weightless in the dream. All is and isn't at the same time. A cloak pulled from this world reveals, for just a split second, another world behind it. Then back to shock, contradiction, collisions of opposites. A dead horse in the sun, its anus filled with a cyclone of maggots. A putrefying rot thickening in the nostrils, but almost instantaneously relieved by a kid walking to market with a basket of spearmint. Now a bamboo flute sounds a lilting melody from a worker resting under a haystack. But only for a short while do the ears savor it. On the topmost stairs of Swayambhunath an argument is going on. Under Buddha's eyes a drunk woman stumbles.

Thunk
       thunk
              thunk . . .

Her body thuds down a dozen concrete steps as her mate glibly stands there, himself drunk, propping his body against a steel rail. Further along, in a sun-warmed courtyard, a spinning wheel purrs softly while on the street a puppy shrieks, its head crushed under a cart wheel deliberately rolled back and forth by child pranksters.

Filled by despair, I weigh on my surroundings, fall face down into the murdered dream, look up, follow a hummingbird's path into a jetliner whose enormous wings shine like a raptor's. The plane, seemingly navigated by its own instinctive power, slowly grows invisible in the cold light of its solitary course. A giant hawk with humans in its stomach. Passengers lost in abandonments, privacies, illusions of separateness; or locked behind masks: some toothless, some hairy, some lipsticked, some washed, some dirty, some veiled, some bandaged, some angry, some fearful, some vulnerable or laughing or ready to cry.

A sound, now, from up high. Not so high as the plane nor the hummingbird, but from an open upstairs window in a whitewashed wall. The window perfectly frames a musician's cocked arm sliding a bow across a violin. A soothing raga flows above the drone of an accompanying harmonium. A raga whose complex vibrations darken the clouds and draw rain.

I take refuge beneath the musicians' window as thick, cold drops pelt the red earth. They bounce from a snail's back, turn the hides of grazing bulls into shining ingots, fill the mouths of violets with tiny pools of reflected sky. Over Swayambhunath a double rainbow shines. Buddha is pleased. The question mark beneath his eyes turns right side up. A burro stammers a long drawn-out hee haw.

From across the road, between the jeweled foliage of an overgrown garden, a child stares, as fascinated with me as I am with the world, her head propped doll-like on an elbow on a blue window sill. Everything—the snail, the grazing bulls, myself, the raindrops—is set to stage by a master choreographer. A nuptial here. A shift in the heavens. A shift in the body's blood stream. The bridesmaid smiles from her blue frame. The violinist reveals himself, rising to the window as he brings his raga to a close. Beaming a toothless smile, he bows with violin outstretched, white shirt billowing like a sail in the wind.

"Namaste . . ."

❌

Darkness.

The girl across the way, there no more. The violinist, gone. Had they been allotted only a few frames in this reeling cinema of karma that fills experience with those we are supposed to meet?

Chaos, fertile silence this late afternoon.

Clear water falling across the world, ionizing the double secrets of what the eye thinks it sees, and the awakened dream filling the streets. I am only an approximation of myself, called to bring together this experience in a foreign land—the monkeys silhouetted in the moonlight I mistook for chanting monks last night; or this afternoon's revelations shining like pebbles under the sea—into meaning; song. In my quest for knowledge I live every doubt, tumbling through the trap door of humanity's folly. The mind tries to order the eye, and in so doing separates the self from what is seen. Kathmandu returns the gaze to the immediate, gathers together all terrors, all disbelief and sends the head—throbbing with blood—into unknown stars.

A path, ever elusive, calls us forward.

Why else travel? Except to live in life what we seek spontaneously underneath the skin: release, unity with mystery, marriage with the missing figure at our side, the rib from which we were born. Companion . . . Avatar . . . Dancer who breaks the veil of the dream. She who will remain standing in my outline when I dissolve into smoke, chlorophyll, candle flame and rain.

▨

THE WAY TO THORANG LA

Annapurna.

From childhood on I've craved this mountain. As a boy I fell to sleep scanning a National Geographic map of India pinned to my bedroom wall, one of many maps my father saved from his stint in the army. In the northern kingdom of Nepal, sinuous isobars broke into chiseled cartography indicating cirques, ice fields and ragged ridges. Nightly, I walked those ridges, hoping to meet the people, to see how they lived and what they saw from their windows. But before any people, villages or high peaks appeared, sleep overtook me. To wake again was to dream of visiting those faraway lands.

Once, my mother read me a paragraph from a large book about world wonders. It described the Himalayas as "mountains still growing." I saw myself standing in a field, watching peaks slowly rise into the clouds before my eyes. Another summer, rummaging through a neighbor's Goodwill box, I found Maurice Herzog's *Annapurna*. Inside were two striking photos: one showed Annapurna's crest, a jagged sweep of pink ice called "The Sickle." The other showed a man with pick and rucksack suspended in mid air from an impossible cliff. He dangled in a transparent world, nothing between him and heaven except his own will; nothing to break his fall if he lost his grip. It was death or the sublime.

One day I took from my rock collection a prized crystal resembling Annapurna's summit. Between the roots of our backyard lemon tree I buried it as far as my ten-year-old arm would reach. To this day I wonder what impulse provoked that act. Perhaps to bury the "mountain" was to hide the dream so that it couldn't be taken from me.

Thirty-odd years later, I am here, not with the intent of climbing Annapurna's 26,500-foot throne, but of circumambulating the mountain. Or at least to make it to Thorang La, a lofty pass between the arid Manang Valley and the lost world of Mustang. Though I shall not be hanging from a cliff like the man in the photo, I nevertheless give serious regard to hiking up the 17,770-foot pass. Dehydration, loss of morale, altitude sickness, slipping backwards on a heel: any of these could mean walking two weeks in, only to have to be carried out—destination unreached.

Adventure does not drive me. Nor reason. Rather, something in the genes alchemically combines with impulse and sets the feet forward. To be called into the world's wideness; and further. Into thin, flint-scented air. The oxygenless realm of creaking stone, prismed light, large-knuckled pillars of ice. Heights that constantly change as loss of gravity challenges the grip.

Two days ago I was on a bus, a jalopy with wired-together headlights and taped window cracks, riding seven hours out of Kathmandu over a potholed road, west towards Pokhara. A French man with a bottle of rum, curved pipe and newspaper sat across from me, a little tipsy. Next to him was a tribal woman with vermilion dye adorning the part in her hair, looking like a bleeding hatchet wound. She smoked a bummed cigarette, occasionally reversing the ashes into her mouth.

Each time the bus rounded a precarious curve, puffs of hashish rose from the rear seats. Three wacky Germans dressed as sadhus would fire up their chillums and slowly the burning pipes would be passed to the front of the bus. A group of Tibetan monks smiled politely and passed a chillum forward. Some of the passengers refused. Others, after all these years, had their first hit. A rather straight British couple in their late thirties, obviously tense and on the verge of break up, found one of the chillums in their hands. The man, with his folded stack of maps and penciled schedule, frowned at the woman. The woman, using the occasion to bolster her independence, took an overpowering draw and relaxed into ecstasy for the rest of the journey. One by one, at isolated river forks and trail heads, backpackers, imitation sadhus, tribal people, and tourists carrying solar-powered video cameras were dropped off. In the stifling tumble-down town of Dumre, I too stepped off. From there the journey began.

※

The Marsyangdi River sets my course: a turquoise gleam through rice paddies and subtropical woods. Bridges sway. Trails split. Stones creak. Jaws pop. The river softens resistances as she maintains a steady course through the darkest chasms, singing with an unbroken rhythm of whitewater that never leaves my ears. Down low, the Marsyangdi Valley is inhabited by Brahmin shopkeepers, Newar and Chhetri farmers. Their thatch-roof stone houses are plastered with soft coats of white mineral and sienna mud, windows and doors bordered with black dots and triangular hexagrams. Here and there I notice pairs of whitewashed votive stones placed in the rice fields.

The valley narrows. A few days of fairly level route through farm plots and scattered banyans, and the feet relax into overdrive. One afternoon, though, a sudden bend reveals a steep switchback ascent: five hours through nettles and screwpine, over broken rock, across badly-sagging suspension bridges. Sprays of bamboo fringe wet cliff sides—delicate from afar, dark and massive up close—creaking like masts of ancient ships. Fields thin. Clouds pile against the Himalayas. Rice terraces give way to orchid canyons and precarious terraces of corn, peas, buckwheat. A hawk circles. Jays chatter through evergreens. A tiny wren spreads her tail, baring a snowy rump. Instantly the distant peaks are brought closer.

In a high glacier-cut gorge, the first Gurung settlements appear. Tribal people with Tibetan features, animist-Buddhist-Hindu mix. Mountain farmers, herders, soft-spoken innkeepers much different in physique and character than the willowy stock of fair-skinned Aryans below. Flat stone roofs replace vertical thatch. Gaudy Chinese thermoses printed with dragons adorn lantern-lit kitchens. Sand-polished brass cookware lines wooden shelves above hand-sculpted mud hearths set with pots of boiling potatoes and rice. A few homes sport cast-iron stoves fired with dung and sticks. One stove has a tin door with a swastika cut into it, flame tongues leaping through.

In a musty lodge I order "Om Lit. Sweet Fit Hers" and sit on a Tibetan rug on an earthen embankment molded right into the wall. A splintered door leads to the rear yak corral. On it, a poster of Sylvester Stallone. Above him, the Dalai Lama. An open window frames steep cliffs, silvered by sheets of water, darkened with lichen. On the lower slopes whole forests have been hacked away. The topsoil is probably far out in the Bay of Bengal by now. A churning micaceous ooze dirties the Marsyangdi here. Rains have dislodged a wooden shrine and carried it head-first into her milky waters.

Through the mists rise Lamjung and Manaslu—23,000 and 26,000 feet. No soil to be owned or fought over up there. Only fluttering snow banners wrapped around wind-sculpted peaks like ribbons around May poles. Whenever my pace becomes tedious the eye is lightened by those summits. The body gains momentum in their presence.

※

From six to ten thousand feet, the trail switchbacks. The river pours over an enormous bowl of slick granite, miles across. Cloud forest thins. Moss-hung hardwoods are replaced by birch, dry air. A sharp eastward turn here: into the Manang Valley. Ice scraped and wind scoured. South: the Annapurna massif—chilly glaciers broken into seracs. Diamond light shifting from crinkled snow patterns and permanently-frozen waterfalls. North: a lower range of jagged 20,000 foot peaks crisscrossed with trade routes into Tibet.

At times I am slowed by wheezing porters around whom I must pass. Young men, teenage wives. Barefoot, poorly clad. Bent under kilos of cooking fuel and tents, rebar, plastic plumbing, roughcut timber and yak meat. They serve bosses and inn keepers in the high country; or attach themselves to Sherpas who direct mountain tours. When they set down their loads for a cigarette break, I speed past. There is a silent exchange of looks. They check my shoes and wristwatch, ask the time, note the weight of my pack. I check their baskets and tumplines, thin cotton clothing, amulets and jewelry. Sometimes the women turn their faces, automatically anticipating a camera, or a question which they can't understand or don't want to be asked. Sometimes they hold up their children and ask for money. Or chocolate. Or pens. An old habit, and tiresome.

※

Walking is my home, has been for days. No roof, no walls as I move from room to room, rice paddy to rain forest, orchid canyon to arid uplift. It's three weeks, 150 miles, around Annapurna. All the while, two voices speak: one wants never to leave; the other is impatient for Thorang La, the homeward descent back to conveniences like hot showers and comfortable sleep. The closer I approach, the more I realize that the pass is there to test my mind, to reveal its discomforts and impatience. And it's a restless, judgmental mind, indulgent in complaints when schedules aren't met, the rice burnt, or the tea lukewarm and overpriced. A mind which ultimaely must take a back seat. For the body, with its own rhythms and instructions, is in command. Feet, legs, the swing of the arms—all adjust to gravity's pull while the mind teeters, seeking conquests and rewards. Or plays with expectations: how things ought to be rather than what is.

Not unlike zazen, the walk has become a meditation. More specifically, it has become *kinhin,* a walk done between sitting which is, in Robert Aitken's words, "halfway between the quality of attention demanded by sitting and the quality of attention demanded by the everyday world. You are doing zazen while walking, but you must be careful to keep pace with the person ahead of you." The whole mountain range is a vast zendo, where one sits, walks, sings eats and always confronts, at the most outlandish moments, ridiculous tangles of mind garbage and memory clutter invading the cells.

Deliberately, I have placed placed myself here, just as I would place myself in a zendo, for stillness and heightened concentration. Or simply to forget the self, to accept the self. To struggle with breath counts, to be at ease with the breath. To know someone's next to me, to not know. To become absent of thought, to be shocked by thought—by what's going on inside me.

The pass is in the heart. Already I am high enough to look down on Mars. Shrine to shrine, cairn to cairn, the body acclimatizes, struggling to keep pace with its own shadow. Each morning it readies itself—without indulgence in aches—for the zigzag route marked on the blueprint trekking map which fades a little more each time it is opened to the Himalayan sun.

The body is a walking sutra. As I trek, songs come to my lips, blood throbs in the skull. Storms, resurgences, ancestral memory, the genes of the ichthyosaur, the seeds of the unborn, the words of my fiercest enemy, the wisdom of the ancients: they are inside my limbs and trunk. Lao Tzu's words are agates in a crystal tarn. Bodhi Dharma's meditation wall is an imposing glacier, mottled with debris. Mirabai's bangles clink as starlit frost breaks mountains into shards. Across ancient shorelines, the body daredances, straddles icefalls, follows darkened shadow galaxies into whirling sunbeams. I pause, sip miso, eat seaweed. Collect ammonites, press plants and poems between the page. In any one place I could stop, absorb and remain for a lifetime—just looking. To be called in, and upon arrival be called in again.

▓

Today I find myself remembering the words of two men, both wanderers of spirit and geography, passionate in their beliefs. Asked by an interviewer "What is life's purpose?" Joseph Campbell replied: "Purpose? There is no purpose! We are going nowhere." And, Nikos Kazantzakis, in his diary from a transoceanic and simultaneously interior journey, remarked: "Do not seek friends in the craggy ascent. Seek comrades-in-arms. Be always restless, unsatisfied, unconforming. Whenever a habit becomes convenient, smash it!"

This trek around Annapurna is a wheel symbolic of life's greater pilgrimage between birth and death. The ups, downs, impossibilities that block ascent. Landslides, creaking suspension bridges. Every barrier to mind and body that spirit must overcome. Hunger pains. Unsatisfied love. The unexpected, final embrace with offspring or parent. A last loveworn session with a companion from whom you are about to part. The grinding chatter of ceaseless internal dialogue. The endlesss disappointment created by the illusion that other people are there to make our lives happy. All of these the journey brings to bear.

Spectator, participant. I am the face of everything seen:

Sickness . . .

A household of scantily-clad children infested with scabies, scratching their armpits and crotches, bleeding in those places. Unable to peel a potato or haul a water bucket without stopping to attend their afflictions.

Old age . . .

A withered grandfather, eyes cloudy, frail body folded into a wicker chair and lifted onto the back of a porter, who—underfed and underpaid—is hired as a barefoot ambulance to deliver the old man a hundred kilometers downhill to the nearest treatment center.

Death . . .

The smoke-tinged doorway of a dirt-floor hovel: a corpse, meagerly wrapped in unaffordable cloth, waiting to be borne on a makeshift stretcher and hauled to the final fire.

Such as it is, this human condition. Birth, death, renewal. The joys, the cruelty in between. The ability to make love, to procreate, to celebrate. The ability to rape, fire missiles, dismember.

"What is meant by happiness? To live every unhappiness. What is meant by light? To gaze with undimmed eyes on all darknesses."

Kazantzakis again.

🔀

Steepening trail. The porter's bare legs up ahead. Strain of muscle, pump of air. His mouth open, asking for two breaths instead of one. My own, yawning, yawning—until every thought swallows itself, wakes empty of discourse, becomes mineral, etched by acids, framed by stars and pressurized rock. I feel my vertebrae flex to fit the ups and downs of the mountain, aware of the torso's cumbersome, upright position. Better a lithe shape—gills and fins to propel me through through these ancient fossil reefs.

🔀

Braga.

A hamlet perched at 11,000 feet on a barren south-facing crag. From here Annapurna is overpowering. As in picture books of youth, mystical shreds of snow spin like arms from her sides. "She who embraces the world," the villagers say. And everywhere they've paid tribute. River stones carved with mantras are piled into cairns. Block-printed flags release prayers over fields and homes. High on a rocky hill, the *gompa* stands out—its flat roof snapping with Buddhist banners, its monastic sanctuaries overlooking Braga's maze of stick-and-stone dwellings. A path up to it zigzags between prayer wheels, sun-heated rock walls, piles of kindling and fodder, puddles of urine. Each simple, squat dark-roomed hut accomodates humans and animals alike.

Around a corner, a stately woman in Tibetan dress combs out her shimmering hair to dry. She smiles shyly, then covers her face with her long black bangs and ducks behind a notched-pole ladder. The scene takes me back to Hopi: similar people, similar architecture, life lived close to the clouds. A few more paces, and I come across a lump of dirty rags—breathing, warming in the sun. An old man. Forlorn, bony, mouth caked with spittle, eyes shut with mucous. He can't see but knows I'm here. Knows my race, my transient state. And waves me away. I look backwards through the stick-and-stone village toward Annapurna, its crystal presence. "*Anna,*" sustenance. "*Purna,*" goddess. The mountain that has drawn me from the other side of the world; the mountain into whose arms this old man was born, upon whose slopes his seeds were planted, from whose soil his wife, children and animals were nourished.

That I should be given so many images of death as I travel, is to receive a gift: the recognition of my own mortality. Stranger here, stranger back home, I walk to rid of accumulation, regain perspective, become small in the shadow of a massif larger and more mysterious than anything dreamed. If there be a duty connected with this journey, it is to give significance to it. To ascend each switchback not by foot but by the

128

power of a humble song.

※

Up top, into the dark, old gompa. Odors of rancid butter. Dust. Burning candles. *Chang*—barley beer. Monks and lamas beating yak-skin drums, crashing cymbals, puffing cheeks into long wooden horns. Readying to exit the obscure chamber with an effigy of Mr. Evil: a dough-formed icon sprinkled with home brew, sitting in a tray of damp ceremonial cigarette butts. Lifted to their shoulders, he's carried down the winding path to Braga's grassy village square. There, to the laughter of a hundred shawl-wrapped villagers, Mr. Evil is placed on a stone platform, danced before and riddled with loud bangs from muzzle-loading rifles. Dumped head first into a roaring bonfire, he disintegrates upward, ashes blowing toward Annapurna, lost to the purity of her slopes.

Suddenly, gleeful screams . . .

Masked children by the dozens erupt in volcanic spew from the monastery's open door, each cloaked and waving a pointed stick with which to goose young girls and grannies alike. Tricksters. Baldheads. Cackling hunchbacks. Bulging-eyed jackals. In mad charge, they pour from the *gompa*, down the barren hill, through Braga to taunt spectators who tuck in skirts, pull down hats and rollick with laughter.

In this wild free play, I rid myself of accumulated soot, old battles, gripes, blames and grudges that need not be carried forward. I laugh—and get goosed—by the return of the child self. It's an open-air cathedral without a priest, only the collective self in spontaneous celebration as the sun extinguishes itself behind the Himalayas, crowning Annapurna with chilly spokes of lemon yellow.

�֍

Two days later, 15,000 feet, set camp . . .

Fingers are too cold to eat with when all is through. Close by, porters attend a French trekking party with all the amenities of reclining chairs, portable latrines, gas lanterns, barbecued chicken, Chardonnay and table cloths. After clean up, the Nepalese bed down in their own ragged assortment of tents. All night long the earth shakes with their chronic hacks and a vibrating wheeze that'll surely have their lives by thirty. At midnight a baby cries desperately. At two a.m. there's a sudden sob pushed back into the throat. A man? A woman? Someone in the middle of a nightmare, under a tremendous yoke. Someone for years in the habit of wanting something else, unable to attain it—not even in dreams.

At three a.m. time to rise. Break camp under a cold, thin moon. Strap myself in under my pack, walk a few yards, take a sharp right. Without relief, it's uphill all the way. Feet fall behind themselves, then discover proper rhythm by the light of Pleiades. Thorang La, the pass I anticipated with fear as well as scorn, is invisible. I head for it, but after so much contemplation and preparation the idea of crossing it doesn't matter. The heart slows as it attempts to gauge the climb. It rhythms strangely off key yet perfectly in tune to the degree of ascent. Ultimately the body accepts the thin air, feeds on stellar equations, thrives on endless designs of bronze and violet inside the eye.

Far below, the Dipper stands on end, wobbles and collapses into into a valley of whistling stone . . .

The pass is in the heart. We shall always be crossing it, acclimatizing, gauging the slope. I walk through me, outside myself. Laugh at the specter behind, weep when he stumbles, am startled when his feet lift him from the ground and take flight over a chasm. Clearly, I see that he is both exhausted and uplifted in the darkness, struggling with one foot on solid ground, the other hanging off the edge.

Friends ask "Why climb?" I search for an answer to fit each asker of the question. It always turns up the same. I climb the mountain because, to quote George Mallory who disappeared on Everest, "it is there;" because, as my old friend Nanao wrote, "mountain is myself" and because, as Lucien Devies said in his introduction to Maurice Herzog's *Annapurna*... "It suggests the infinite, but it is not the infinite. In the extreme tension of the struggle toward the summit, the absolute, the universe disappears and drops away beneath us. Space, time, fear, suffering no longer exist. We are strangely calm—not the calm of emptiness, but the heart of action itself. Then we know with absolute certainty that there is something indestructible in us, against which nothing shall prevail."

Three hours later, the top . . .

Cold, soaked with sweat, I absorb the sunrise. Small faraway orb. Violet-green atmosphere. Short breaths. Quick 5-7-5 steps around a whitewashed cairn whose fluttering prayer flags transform the wind into a mantra. A prayer of gratitude for my body's health, for all who have made this journey possible. Food that has fed, fire that has warmed, air that has sustained me. A prayer that each and every creature be given strength to overcome suffering; that those who uproot the lives of families and the life of the earth may awaken to their ignorance.

Time halts at this summit. Becomes a concentric ripple inside the eye. When it opens, it opens with the very first moment in the world. In it I am simply here, a consecrated semblance set to flame. Truth is beauty, the elemental reality that surrounds. Doubt is that ragged gap, flushed with sunlight, through which I've hiked. From peak to peak, snow banners feed infinity with fine sparkles of jeweled dust. It is here that I begin, humble and pedestrian, at crest—becoming light with the climb.

※

MEDITATIONS FROM PHRA NANG

The sleek, pearl-blue Mercedes bus growls out of Bangkok into Thailand's storm-ripped lower peninsula. In the aftermath of a cyclone, palm trunks and tin roofs litter the highway. Flood waters rise precariously in the beams of four powerful headlights. Occasionally I recognize a splintered temple half submerged in swirling flotsam, its pointed eaves rearing into the soggy night like black flames.

Inside the bus, perfumed attendants distribute hot towels and boxed snacks, atomize the air, and cover us with blankets in fully reclining seats. Pneumatically-sealed from the havoc outside, we relax to a video player illuminating a four-foot screen above the driver's head. Melodramatic Thai movies run all night with love scenes translated into eclectic English subtitles:

```
             Am I feminism?
     Take your knife away. We are the same boat.
             Does it worth it for a girl?
     Let's play one to one.  Call me when you are boring.
         After wake up I feel shaky, like rain.
          I like crazy because you very tasty.
                 You can afford me?
        You are peanuts. I pay half expenses.
```

I drift, then wake to a low yellow moon between bloated clouds. At dawn, the iodine sky burns through tinted glass. Steep, bulbous limestone hills rise through heavy drapery of jungle, waterfalls pouring between misty nodes. At the end of the line is a seaside town on a narrow inlet littered with lopsided fishing boats, orchid and Naples yellow, fading in tropical heat. On a flimsy boardwalk over the oil-splotched lagoon—where motorized canoes arrive from picture-puzzle islands dotting the sea—a few of us hire a boatman for Phra Nang, a get-away cove on a peninsula half an hour away. Meanwhile, a breakfast of crab claws served with boiled bananas in salty-sweet coconut milk.

❖

Thailand's southwest coast, its James Bond islands and coral reefs, is mecca for pan-Asian travelers seeking rest after Nepalese treks, hepatitis in India, broken romances, endless passport hassles and bouts with undigestible food. Like a temporary release from samsara, the Andaman Sea beckons the backpack vagabond. Those from India find it a godsend just to be left alone. No questions, no pestering, no stare-down contests, no clang of puja bell and off-key 4 a.m. loudspeaker hymns. Those from Nepal experience nirvana by simply shedding smoky sweaters and polypropylene gear, getting naked and snorkling for days on end in underwater luxury.

❖

Evening.

Fuchsia rays spread from the ocean's rim. A single planet rises in the west, its emerald beam riding a wave across Phra Nang cove up to the beach and over my toes. A scampering primate chatters in the mangroves. Drift of lemon grass. Fresh catch from a landed skiff. Hornbills in the palm trees. Shapely plastic goddesses smiling from wooden spirit houses—miniature replicas of Thai temples—perched on posts overgrown with bromeliads.

A tang of incense perfumes the air. But it is not incense. Behind the mangroves, numerous hardwoods have been poached, their stumps left smoking. By king's order, local mills should be sawing only trees imported from Burma. World news has given Thailand a coveted position lately: a "model" country that has banned logging on a national scale. What is overlooked is that the king had no other choice. There's nothing left to cut. The upshot of the ban: relentless pressure on Burma and Laos to clear cut and sell to Thai mills.

In a bamboo eatery along the beach, I take a chair at a table set with mosquito coils and plastic lotus buds. I've promised to reflect, to review my travels. But there's a futile sense that I've already said what's to be said. Light years might pass before what's been seen and what it means fully reveals itself. For now, I dry saltwater from my skull and document a receding hairline with a gentle stroke of the comb.

A rooster flaps and crows on the next table.

A waitress—looking so much like a teenage *apsara* stepped from her spirit house—sets down an exquisite plate of steamed cockles, fish buttered with garlic and transparent noodles over basil. I indulge, watching twilight spread like lavender ink into rice paper, examining today's beachcombed treasures: sand dollar, spiral conch, iridescent sand beetle.

But they engage me only briefly. I am an unhappy man in paradise tonight. Worried about the planet. Deluded by the unpredictable human mind. Its need to violate, plunder, pit itself against nature. Perhaps it's the presence of the smoking stumps, the last of Southeast Asia's forests shredded into fiber board and foundation forms. Or maybe it's the Bangkok Post reporting China's billion-dollar arms trade with Burma's junta for teak and minerals. Or Phnom Penh's continued war—the irony of soldiers barricading themselves behind piled craniums from the last war. Or the leaking boat spilling sixty Vietnamese to their deaths, while across the date line a 23 year-old Vietnamese refugee wins sixty million dollars in a New York lottery.

If I consider these times of violence and resignation as my fate, despair invades me. But if I view them as a wake-up call, the door opens with possibilities. Doubt is the great catalyst that brings the mind to a heightened state of examination. Dangling from one of several connoisseur tea bags printed with obscure quotations (purchased before leaving New Delhi) I found this statement by Henry James. It's now pasted on the last page of my notebook:

We work in the dark, we do what we can, we give
what we have, our doubt is our passion and our passion
is our task. The rest is the madness of art.

I think of the apostle Thomas putting his finger into Christ's wound after he'd risen, his need to *feel*—not just believe or accept—if his master's death and resurrection had really happened. Perhaps the Great Doubter is the one most apt to be carried by a state of essential wonder back to square one, the base from which one feels life and responds to it with the heart. Doubt opens the door to truth, and that word—so connected with *trust* in the English language—holds a different meaning for each of us. For some, truth implies a primal beauty that affirms life—right at the very time in human history when our nature seems obsessed with destroying life.

I go back to that moment, rounding Annapurna at the crest of Thorang La. A vast, ethereal panorama where the world stood still, the heart chakra, opened and a voice inside me exclaimed: "Truth is beauty, the elemental reality that surrounds." *Beauty!* Something essential to the psyche that we've lost touch with. A state of wild delight in which all beings are revealed in the perceiver's eye as cosmically married. A shimmering interconnection where every leaf, atom, star, aphid, spawning salmon, molten eruption and lapiz-faced glacier hums in the perceiver's head with a kind of musical, muscular movement.

James Hillman reminds us that "Beauty is an *epistemological* necessity; it is the way in which the gods touch our senses, reach the heart and attract us into life." He says the "main aim of all depth psychologies is to recuperate the lost soul, to recover our lost aesthetic reactions . . . the luster of each particular event."

Beauty, then, as recognition, wonder, honor—of Earth's body, our own flesh, the amazement of things as they are, appearing, disappearing and reappearing before us every day. The smile of the Divine, the forever in the ephemeral. The goodness, the goddess. The immortal *gasp* rooted in the soul's primary response before thought reaction gets in the way. The Face of things revealed by haiku poets, sans elevated visionary beauty, idealized perspective or philosphical constructions.

Haiku master Basho called it *karumi*, lightness. A particular state of being in which seer and seen are inseparable, because if self and object were separable, one's poetry would be a subjective counterfeit, an understanding, refinement or correction of the commonplace. How much of our daily existence *is* counterfeit! Standing apart from the world, we are cast from the garden, we lose eternity. The eternity of now. In one of his haiku Basho invited us to:

Come, see
real flowers
of this painful world

※

Hungry for world news, I read while I eat. About India's attempt to nationalize Hindi and force it on the subcontinent. About China imposing its language on Tibet—and government policies as well. The men in power are divided from their actions. Unable to live without excess, control and riches, it is no wonder they want everyone to speak one language. Language of commerce. Language of war. Language that drifts, confuses, becomes obscure with policies designed to keep words from meaning, citizens from thinking. Amazing, the energy put toward creating conflict, and the time spent resolving subsequent tension.

Large scale, small scale, secular or religious, the need to convince, manipulate and divide seems to infest our daily living. Today a born-again Christian tossed a purposeful Frisbee into the lap of a topless sunbather. An excuse to proselytize.

"Do you know the Lord?"
His rehearsed smile was shunned, thank goodness.

The little *apsara* walks up with a tray of beer. I select one whose gold label depicts a lion chasing a star. After a swig, the Bangkok Post is open again. This time a story about a foreigner arrested at a Thai beach resort after going off the edge in the name of charity. The headlines:

TOURIST BLINDS HIS OWN MOTHER

How? By setting fire to her traveler's checks and thrusting them into her face. Why? Consumed with religious fervor, he wanted the family fortune donated to south Thailand's typhoon victims. Overwhelmed by his threats, the mother gave in, asking only that she be spared enough money to return to Austria. Furious, the son soaked their savings with lighter fluid and smothered her in flames. Afterwards he showed no remorse. "Mother always had a hard time giving up worldly possessions to help the poor."

※

Shouts of children. My handwriting stops.

They've gathered on the beach while my nose has been in the Post. Their slippery bodies, lit by the bright planet rising in the west, frolic in evening dance. Splashing in the shallows, they raise exuberant arms towards a fishing skiff motoring in from sea. When the boat is anchored and their fathers sort the evening catch, the children intensify their song, as if to praise the God in every silvery fin and tail still jumping with life. Gracefully, waves roll and break with foamy applause. Around the skiff in a circle the kids cup hands, dredge the warm waters, bringing to surface phosphorescent plankton, millions of diamond bodies that, when agitated, divide into a million more. Now a mother calls. And another. The little ones skitter across the beach like sandpipers.

My eyes follow back to the planet. Thunderheads pile beneath it. A storm brews. I am in the eye of God's whirlpool. Burning, creating form as I burn. Flesh expanding with branches of heat. Roots feeding from an incomprehensible spirit who cries: "It is not only the rain forest, elephant and starving child that must be saved. It is the imagination." What Lorca calls the "Duende." What Mirabai calls the "Unnavigable Sea." What Kazantzakis identifies as "an ethereal, vehement Eros."

Theory isn't the answer. Nor passive speculation. The supplications I lift into thunderous nights fall futilely into breaking waves to be returned to my feet. I am left to perceive and confirm on my own. To bend with God under weight of fear and daily labor. Tens of thousands of pundits in India collect money and spill milk on lingams, while poverty's face moans, recites and struggles to find enough rupees to please a fat, invented pantheon. The priests are not naked enough. They do not dance, but stand aloof blessing themselves while coins fill their baskets. Theirs is not the joy of Phra Nang's children. Their sacred lingams are not powerful and grand like the erect limestone islands teaming with birds in the Andaman Sea.

The fishing skiff bobs gently in its cove. The plankton brought to surface by the children evaporate toward heaven and reincarnate as stars. Each star is given shape by praise of lifted arms, bodies dancing around a teakwood skiff, voices raised joyously in the tropical night. In turn, stars pollinate our world, sending carbon into the body, filling Earth with the "dust of creation" hinted at in the Vedas. The beaming planet overhead permits song to sing from open mouths, provides forward energy leading rivers to oceans, swimmers back to surface from rapturous depths.

I recline on the beach, tinier than the grains of sand that combine to provide my bed. What is spoken teletypes out into zodiacal shapes. In sleep each of us casts a net. Down it sinks, into caverns of mental drift. It's the fire, the heat of midnight's catch, the twilight praise of naked bodies that we inherit while in dream. Absorbed by nocturnal glide, we feed on beams disconnected from the world's boundaries, a book escaping as it opens, a wave that breaks in vocal flame—this world a replica of that one beyond: the infinite dance that dances now and ever fast surrounds.

※

A FOREST WAT, SOUTHERN THAILAND

Green soaks the eye. The Incarnation of Mercy and Compassion guards the gate. She pours Elixir upon the world and bathes its wounds. Beyond her, a stairway leads up through the jungle and down into a womb-like amphitheater lush with virgin forest untouched by loggers. Within its bowl of sheer, limestone cliffs carbon dioxide effervesces from leaf hairs. Orchids, air plants, steamy vines of chlorophyll weave into sun ladders. The eye blinks, dazzled with a potent dispersal of emerald light.

In this sanctuary, Buddhist monks and nuns make their homes in separate communities, sleeping in tiny thatched bamboo huts with tin roofs known as *kutis*. Each kuti is raised from the forest floor on four wooden legs set in crocks of water to prevent the invasion of unwanted creatures. Each has a small porch covered with woven bamboo where the meditator sits on a firm cushion facing a dripping grotto or a small, metal icon of the Fasting Buddha.

Inside, the kuti is deliberately sparse. One never sleeps in total comfort but makes do on a tiny floor that hardly permits a full stretch. The only lifestyle lighter is that of India's wandering sadhu. Possessions are few: broom, candle, toiletries, sewing kit, teapot, a saint's picture pasted with votive foil. A makeshift clothesline droops with stream-washed tunics: faded squares of brown, red or saffron drying like abstract paintings in the moist sun.

Day begins early for these Theravada Buddhists. In the dark, dressed in robes and thongs, they make way to the central meditation hall where

145

they chant the Pali scriptures. At daybreak they parade single file to a nearby village, alms bowls extended to receive offerings of fruit and rice. Then back to the *wat*—the monastic complex—for shared tasks of weeding, water hauling, washing, sawing a wind-fallen giant, path sweeping and preparing the noon meal, last of the day.

Twelve hours of meditation follow. Not "meditation" in the sense of its Latin root: *meditatus*, to ponder, to concentrate; but in the sense of its Pali root: *jhana*, which implies a relaxed effortlessness where one calms the mind and opens the heart, no separation between knower, knowing and known. There are many forms of meditation: private, communal, sitting, walking or working. Long periods of quiet allow for reading, studying and frequent interviews with the abbot who often mirrors one's doubts and probing, always returning the seeker to the practice, the investigations.

"Still crave? Clinging to anything?"

"Yes . ."

And it's back to the leaf garden. Sweeping paths. Cleaning the mind. Pruning fear, desire, runaway ambitions that provoke imbalance or harsh actions towards others. Piling anger in kindling stacks. Transforming it into the fire of wisdom that enables one to overcome prejudice and ego addictions. Every ease, every discomfort is felt here. You know when you are listening, not listening. Present or drifting, tranquil or yearning. If you are sweeping, are you fully engaged in that task, or sweeping with one eye checking to see if anyone else is sweeping? Are you putting things in order "for" someone, or surrendering to the act, sans benefits or rewards?

※

Sundown.

A few villagers enter the wat for evening chanting. Afterwards there may be storytelling, discussion of an upcoming festival or plans for building repairs. Then back along hard-packed clay paths through dripping trees to the kutis by candle light.

Like Burma, Laos, Cambodia and Vietnam, Thailand is known for its Theravada Buddhists, the prevalent branch in Southeast Asia. Within this branch exist the Insight Masters, forest monks who acknowledge the heart as the seat of the mind, and spend years perfecting contemplative life under teachers who are direct heirs of Buddha's doctrine. To these Insight Masters arrive seekers: a lay person leaving family or employment for a few weeks to fulfill religious obligation; a lifetime initiate who, as an orphan, was brought to the monastery to be fed, sheltered and educated; or a student on leave from a university whose classes served only to prepare him for a future of conformity, upmanship, power and money.

Nothing could be further from this than monastic life. Here one has no income, does not tangle in theory or abstractions and is taught to question everything society has systemized for the benefit of the elite and the yoke of the poor.

"Waiting for reincarnation?" the abbot asks.
"Or actually living in the reality your body inhabits?"

He points not to a future Buddha nor to refuge in a spiritual realm, but to "Buddha Nature" as revealed in the immediate world: the mole on a chin;

147

the morning glory creeping through a window; the bucket squeaking up from a well; the caterpillar climbing a leaf under the Milky Way. Meditation is not purposeful investigation. There is nothing to understand.

"When cold, say cold. When hot, say hot."

Sit for awhile. Feel body drip rain and forest ooze sweat. Let the mind reveal its turmoil, thoughts blow free and names sink to the bottom. See directly into the truth of the moment without opinion. Then the world will reveal itself without background or foreground, inside or out, this or that.

"Store the clear wind in a mindless cup."

The abbot grins. The words from his wide, moon-shaped face surprise the seeker newly arrived from a busy society where reason is the code, change is resisted, the king isn't questioned and the self exists to be pleased. Bowl. Robe. Stone. Thatch. Embrace simplicity, reduce encumbrances and be reminded how much time is wasted in thinking, scheming, worrying or anticipating tomorrow. Here, one is expected to be present. Do what needs to be done: clean the latrine, rinse the rice, rake the gravel, wring the laundry, chant the sutras.

"But not too much chanting," the master laughs.
"Or you might pass through paradise."

Side by side monks, nuns—void of age, creed or the rank enjoyed in the outer world—are an inseparable body. Yet, the abbot provides each individual with a question, not an answer, to ponder.

"When the Many are reduced to One,
to what is the One reduced?"

�֎

A stream makes a low, bass-fiddle sound where it curves and eddies into
a vortex of leaves and mottled sun. Here is a platform with a clay cistern
for bathing. I scoop water, crouch, scrub. One hand reaches easily around
the body's entire span. Then—*splash!*—into the cold stream for a rinse.
Off I am carried, feeling its depth, probing its quality, skimming, diving,
relaxed enough to flow through stone. Upward, then, I evaporate into a
cloud. Down again—*splash!*—as rain. Time is a tenseless wheel. The
universe kinetic, full of surprise. One day wake, rise and I am no longer
observing the world. It has its eye on me.

Very simply, the monastery is a place to slow down. Swaying trees, wind
dancing through creaking bamboo: these aerate the mind, humidify it,
keep it cool. One observes personal experience as continuous rising and
vanishing of thought and sensation. When it is time to make the alms
rounds, the monks file into the world with new sets of eyes. Visiting the
village cremation grounds, walking city streets where lepers beg, addicts
seek their fix, and the sick fill understaffed hospitals, the Thai Buddhists,
like the sannyasins of India, become direct witnesses to the truth of
impermanence.

✖

Today I visit a favorite spot. Mineral-stained palisades rise above the
jungle into precipitous, purple rock castles imprinted with fossil
constellations. Under a natural overhang is painted a life-size Buddha. He

149

sits, one palm up and out extended in the "fear not" gesture; the other over knee, fingers touching earth in silent honor. To Buddha's right is a glass booth. Inside it, a human skeleton faces outward with an eery, toothless smile. Stepping closer, I discover an ant parade filing up the glass carrying a dead centipede heavenward in a long, ceremonial funeral march. To Buddha's left a grandfather clock ticks, its brass pendulum hypnotically reminding the viewer of back and forth human schedules.

In front of Buddha, skeleton, and clock the abbot sits on a gold pillow and gives discourse to the *sangha*, a congregation who listens cross legged on a marble platform amid the greenery. The abbot—cloaked in ochre robe, right arm and shoulder bared, head shaved—dusts a mosquito from his neck and beams his usual wide smile.

"Are you listening to what is said?
 Or busy forming a yes or no?"

Silence. A bird lands on the skeleton cage and pecks at its reflection in the glass. Dark clouds boil in the sky.

"Be still. Attend.
 The truth is too close to see.
 It is dangling from your eyebrows."

Just when you finally settle on your cushion—*Boom!* Thunder roars, wind rises, trees slam, rain lashes the forest canopy. Now what? Leave, stay? Who makes the decisions here? —*Flash!* Stems and leaves, green a second ago, are caught in the colorless white of a lightning stroke. A single, unexpected instant has revealed the world with unsettling intensity, but I have been too preoccupied and have missed it. When showers and sparks clear, there is the abbot still talking, just an ordinary man, like a frog perfectly centered on a stone.

※

Uneasy night tonight. Bed is hard. Body hurts. Even the midnight stars, pinwheeled into cut-glass delicacy, fail to relieve me. A desire, maybe, to be home shaking my body dry like a pup fresh from a stream. By dawn, no stars. The kutis bob like miniature arks in heavy fog. Forest drips. Balcony rails are hidden. Where to turn for support?

※

Today I catch a scooter ride into town for late-afternoon shopping and a night-market snack. Barbecue duck, green papaya salad, mango custard. The place is lively. The Supremes sing from a loudspeaker. Yellow neon dances over steaming food kiosks. As is custom, everyone shares tables. Always an experience, these night markets. Take a seat, and invariably who you are supposed to enjoy as company materializes. Tonight is no exception.

A Thai gentleman in his early sixties pulls up a wooden chair, introduces himself and calls over a rather spicy transvestite waiter — blue lipstick, a sarong printed with pink feathers, and a glittery t-shirt that says, "Rock Me Baby." The gentleman orders a bottle of whiskey and a dozen skewers of *satay*. Two frosty glasses are set before us. A bowl of ice cubes and the usual assortment of peppers and sauces. It's going to be a full evening.

Talkative, spirited, a geologist by profession, the man tells me he was raised in Bangkok, educated at M.I.T., and is now retired, married to his wife for forty years. They live in a seaside home that they themselves designed. It is simple chatter at first. Where I am from. What I do. How long traveling. And would I, upon return to the States, purchase and mail him that Grand Canyon time-chart poster he didn't buy while he was there? But not too far along and we turn to culture, politics, religion. After I tell my story, he begins his.

"After graduation and before finding work in Bangkok, I went to a forest wat near Chang Mai. Our tradition is for men to enter a Buddhist monastery for three months to gain merit for the family. It was expected of me, so I went. I thought I would learn everything needed for right living. But teacher was silent. Forest was silent. I was noisy. Many sounds. Many bad habits looking at me. How to work without cigarette. How to think without cigarette. How to relax without cigarette. Or exist without need to compete or gain reward.

"I was in good disorder. Married, but not knowing who I was married to. Out of school but still thinking like I was in school. Cleverly educated, but what had I learned? Too many ideas printed on me. I was their slave. Big frown, unhappy man. Now I was in the middle of a forest, hair shaved, one set of clothes, no possessions. Things were displeasing and I had no wife, no society, no situation to blame. My complications were my own. I carried them with me. My sense of purpose was just something stamped on me by others. Where to work. What to wear. How to relax. How to hide my feelings. How to look ambitious, tell a funny joke, fill silence with words. But not kind words, even for those closest to me. Always words to gain opportunity.

"Several weeks in the forest and I began to relax. I remember one evening after it rained I was walking next to a pond. The path empty, the ground

152

quiet. Just a small spot of sun on the hills. My mind was completely alone. I heard a child call after a goat. I heard birds in the trees and men breaking sticks and burning brush on a slope. I did not feel them as distant or close. At one point, without even realizing, I was on my knees examining a lotus blossom. Inside it was a rain drop like a mirror reflecting sky and forest and me. I was the center of the world!

"When I left the monastery I wanted to change the world. So much violence, so little feeling. Everyone wanting to protect themselves. I remembered my face in the lotus. I thought—if I am at center, and if my teacher is right about 'present reality' meaning at any given moment all reality is present, then I must change myself for the world to change.

"I had been trained to locate oil, develop mines for international corporations. I took the job my father wanted for me and was surrounded by very uninteresting coworkers. This was not M.I.T. and certainly not the monastery! This was my homeland and I was a stranger. Men I worked with were good at making and spending money. But no vigor for life. Just reactions—pettiness. Everybody in suit and tie but living in a completely uncivilized world. Cruel, filled with trickery. 'Challenge' to them meant 'how quickly can I climb the corporate ladder?'

"So I left. Ended up in seismology. Moved the family to Jakarta and was twelve years there, less pay but happier existence. I worked to save rural families from losing their lives in earthquakes. I suppose my lesson was that it is okay to walk into the world with a big vision, but you must also see that shortcomings in the world are shortcomings inside your own self. When you make right whatever blocks you inside, the world will reflect that change. And you can not do this alone. You need a group you can go back to who shares the same idea. People who do not fear questions or the action needed to settle the questions.

"There was a mountain above the wat in Chang Mai. On top was a little temple on the place where a Bodhisattva, in imitation of the Buddha, gave of himself to a needy creature, a tigress whose mate had abandoned her with a litter. Caring for the cubs, feeding them her milk, she was unable to hunt. The Bodhisattva found the mother starving. With no hesitation he held out his arm and allowed her to eat it.

"The ten-kilometer walk to that shrine I will not forget. Villagers working, loading carts, digging water canals, transplanting rice—with such an ease. Meanwhile, pilgrims were always walking up the mountain. Asian people, European people. Once, I overheard two Americans analyzing what the shrine was about. They walked, heads down, talking loudly the whole way. They just wanted to know if the tiger event was real or not.

"And I would say they missed the charm, the teaching of the event. Logic destroys the significance of a miracle. Miracles are to wake people. You get too tired investigating the Bodhisattva story historically or factually. Better to enjoy the metaphor. Think about it with imagination.

"The purpose of walking up that mountain is not really to get to the top. It is to contemplate the virtue of compassion. The Bodhisattva startles you by his extreme act of charity. He is not delaying the opportunity to give by asking 'how do I get food to the tiger,' or wondering 'should I?' Or thinking 'How much will it hurt when I hold out my arm and the tiger bites?'

"Forty years later that mountain is with me. I am still convinced that

154

compassion must be with us daily. Difficult, when I remind myself of how things are in the world. But it is a matter of attention. Practice. What can I change in me that will make a difference? Today, will I be empty enough of obsessions and worries to give to another?

"In Indonesia I saw, the government moving people onto land belonging to natives. Wildlife killed, streams poisoned, natives forced by big business to cut their own forests. In my own country I see deception, smiles hiding pain. In Cambodia, fighting. In Burma, repression. My government contradicts itself—denouncing Rangoon's dictator, then buying fish, trees, oil. How many of us return from a monastery where they teach Buddha's way, then stand back while students are shot, nuns raped or monks tortured by police masked as monks who spy on resistance communities? All the while Rangoon publishes 'democracy through discipline' propaganda. 'Military protects motherland from riotous destruction.' Things like that.

"In the face of events like these, especially if you travel and you have open eyes, there is always room to ask: 'What is the most important teaching I will take home with me?'"

※

Again, the rain.

Violet-gray streaks cloak and reveal the landscape like a Japanese woodblock print whose slanted rain shifts to expose a cliff, a temple, a tumbling cascade or a miniature traveler lost amid mountains whose power and beauty is hazed by storm. I hurry through the forest, poncho leaking. There's the empty abbot's seat, everything drenched. There's the sad gleam of the clock pendulum, hardly visible in water falling so heavily now that it creates a pounding silence from which rises anger, despair and hope—that monasteries like this will not be merely protected or preserved but recognized for what they are: the embodiment of a possibility for harmony between human beings.

Under the open porch of a vacant kuti, I take shelter. A gecko is here too, using the leaves of an oleander-like bush for an umbrella. Dumbfounded by the sheer amount of rain engulfing the world, I sit and stare until I no longer engage in scenery but look back into myself. Images step forward. Seething cities. Himalayan moraines. A marble shrine of great beauty and paradox. A man inhaling a cigarette through his forehead. A nun printing prayer flags. Wooden ferris wheels lifting children above snow peaks. Pleiades lighting the slope to Thorang La.

Each image does not come without revelation of others' sufferings. And realization, too, that I have been spinning, bouncing like a stone inside a tumbling machine—becoming polished, yes. But in a dark and mysterious vacuum, a world so bizarre and unknown, filled with so many ungraspable edges, that I have had no time to stop. Now the machine slows, offering possibility for reflection.

Drenching water washes me into memory. A sandy beach along the Pacific where I held a shell to my ear as a young boy, listening to sonar rhythms vibrate from a hermetic creature's empty home. That moment contained this one: man on porch, rain hissing inside his ear; just as this moment contains that: child on beach, ocean's roar inside his ear. From there, no great leap to Phra Nang's beach kids frolicking in their starry cove; to Jaisalmer's street actors coping with a wind-blown stage; to the charcoal princess leading me to the stone hermaphrodite in Varanasi.

Always, when travels were most chaotic and the mind in conflict, the presence of children brought balance. Their animated passion and curiosity for life revealed the state of unselfconsciousness so many of us seek to regain.

Only now, in this sanctuary designed for introspection, do I see through those children into my own childhood. There is one moment, repressed for decades, that has to do with the geologist's talk of the Bodhisattva and the tiger. Compassion. The teaching I want to return with into the world. But where did it first arise in my own life? What incident?

Boyhood school days, third grade . . .

A classroom smelling of chalk dust and bagged lunches. A nun, very tall, dirty spectacles. Long, black unwashed garment. A rude and fiercely dictatorial presence, wholly unlike the open-armed woman in flowing blue—the one I loved so much who smiled at me from her niche inside the church. Why was the lady at school who was supposed to be my teacher dressed in black not blue? Why did she frown instead of smile and not extend her arms in the gesture of embrace?

As she sat grading papers, I looked up from my books and wondered who she was. Great confusion arose between the Blessed Lady on her altar, my mother in her apron at home, and the fierce lady dressed in black at school. One lunch period I sat on a bench, lonely for my familiar refuge under the backyard lemon tree. In my distress, half of my peanut-butter sandwich slipped from my lap to the ground. Uneatable, I tossed it over the fence.

The lady in black caught me.

As punishment I had to fetch and eat the sandwich. Red eyed, I looked around in vain for solace. Only one other person witnessed that event. The school custodian—I see him clearly. A man feared, mocked, yet held in curiosity by the children. Small, no necked, large head, impaired speech, he went about his duties stabbing papers on the playground while we kept safe distance.

Once, he was in the classroom, closer than he'd ever been. With grunting noises, wobbling on a wooden stepladder, his stubby fingers unscrewed a light bulb. Muffled laughter. A boy (who later grew up and joined the CIA) aimed a paper wad and bounced it from the man's back. The woman in black looked through her dirty spectacles and dismissed the custodian, not the ruffian. For a long time I was not to see the man, up close or from afar.

One afternoon, walking home from school, there he was. He popped from behind an oleander bush, reached down, picked me up, held me for a few seconds and kissed me on the mouth. Stunned by his own actions, he dropped me and disappeared. I composed myself, continued home, and, upon entering the door, my mother looked down at my pants and asked: "How did you get that grass stain on your knee?"

"Playing kick ball. I fell in the grass."

She frowned, told me to change so she could wash the trousers, and I did—with a long stop in the bathroom to wash my lips with soap. For the rest of my life I denied the incident. But it is vivid now. The man who surprised me, yes. But more so, that first willful act of compassion—which ironically involved a lie. A lie in order to protect a truth. The truth of that man's eyes. The truth of a man whom I perceived

158

to be a suffering individual. Not a harmful person. A lonely one, undeserving of embarrassment or punishment. Had there been violence in the man's eye, the incident might have taken a different turn. As it was, the young boy's perception, unblurred by prejudice, remained untold until now.

�֎

Soaked to the bone, and laughing.

Leaving my refuge, walking into a wet world, meeting monks soaked to the bone, and laughing. Passing big belly Buddha, storm-wet and laughing. Passing rank old skeleton wet in his cage—also laughing. Watching the rain clear, soaked to the bone. Up over the limestone lip, down the stone-paved stairway out of the womb, into a bright world.

Kuan Yin, smiling on her pedestal.
Blessed Lady, pouring her elixir . . .

At a bus stop along the dirt road I hail a lopsided contraption full of people. No sides, outward-facing benches. Step aboard. Conductor lady rattles coins in her metal ticket tube, punches me a fare. With blue puffs of exhaust, we jerk and rattle down the trail. Passengers with nylon bags, cackling hens, pink squid and fruit. They smile, as if having heard my truth, my story.

Where I've been and how far I've come.
They all seem to know.

✖

AIR BORNE

My eye has been pressed to the window for hours now, lost to shifting whorls of stars, the 747's wing blinking regularly in the blackened void, held steady by the weight of its fuel, the angle of its foil. At the first sight of the Southern Cross I tilt my cap, recognizing an old friend winking at me. Five miles below I can barely make out the designs of moonlit whitecaps breaking upon luminous atolls in a dance of hieroglyphs.

The aircraft banks without warning. A plastic cup of Javanese coffee slides gently across my tray. When the plane regains balance and my nose is against the window again, I realize another phenomenon: that I am no longer in a world of right angles, grid of cities, low-ceilinged buildings normalized by the square. My dreams are round, the planet is round, the plane's window is round, and in it is the reflection of my own round face superimposed on the stars above and atolls below. A whole universe is contained in my outline.

My thoughts wander to the desert back home—a petroglyph of a circular face carved almost a thousand years ago by an Anasazi villager. It greets the rising sun from a volcanic bluff overlooking the Rio Grande. Inside the pecked outline of the face are mountains, rivers, zigzag lightning strokes, sprouting corn plants, celestial storms, the prance of bighorn sheep. Whoever inscribed that face must have been deeply connected with the huge curve of grasslands spreading out from the site and back into the imagination where it completed itself in an all-encompassing circle. Each nuance of the exterior cosmos joined with that of the artist's interior cosmos, and the weave—indeed cosmic—was replicated in stone. *Kosmos*: "an ordered, harmonious whole." A "round" feeling (Miles

161

Davis once called his sound "a round sound") as opposed to the broken, unconnected corners of chaos.

Despite the visible urban sprawl of Albuquerque, I always experienced a feeling of solace at that site. Perhaps that is what a "sacred place" is: a particular geography that elevates the beholder with wonder, often reverently or symbolically inscribed, giving rise to what John Muir called "wild delight." An exalted feeling of being connected with everything wild. An animated ecstasy inspiring both reverence and gratitude for the things of the earth.

❋

The tip of Irian Jaya comes into view. Heavy cumuli are piled against its emerald uprise. Probably a lot of smoke from burning rainforests mingled with those clouds too. I switch on the high-intensity bulb overhead and read from my little spiral notebook, a stray thought penned somewhere in the darkness:

"The mind is a feeble animal struggling in the cranium's shell, understanding nothing of the overwhelming edge of dark meeting light. It laughs nervously or permits an occasional muffled howl at the Mystery that surrounds—the Occult Reality that holds neither to truth nor time but to the center of its own cosmic self. What, then, *is* Creation? A giant corolla seeding the eye second by second, hour by hour? And this creature called *me*? Once a simple mammal, all instincts intact, now evolved into a human hypochondriac strapped into a cushioned seat miles above the Pacific floor?"

I slip my notebook back into a shirt pocket, and stand to stretch. A flight attendant pinned with a pair of mythical Garuda wings offers me a cocktail and, with a total stranger, I raise a Bloody Mary toward a ceiling of wallpapered dragons. She smiles, I smile, while toward the cockpit a lavatory door clicks shut. The "Occupied" light flicks on. In the windows, beyond sleeping passengers, the clouds have built into endless opalescence—the great milk sea from which the Hindu gods churned *amrita*, the soul-reviving ambrosia that invigorates searchers as they lose themselves in the maze, the *manna* that sustained the Isrealites in their journey through the wilderness.

"Biak," the pilot announces.

Already I can see bromeliads leafing from tree crotches, painted tigers embellishing sarongs, fireflies landing in the palms of children suckling from their mothers' breasts.

"Would Paul Guaguin feel at home with Nintendo?"

I don't think *that* is the question. Not at all. And it won't get answered, my tipsy tourist—for the pilot has called us all back to our seats and the plane is touching down with burning roulette wheels on the puddled tarmac, 6 a.m. Irian Jaya time.

Shortly, we step down the portable stairs from the giant hulk of the plane and are ushered toward the tin-roofed airport's welcoming committee waiting on polished floors in a stuffy room with an old Dutch wall clock swinging its pendulum above Suharto's portrait. Below him are two sticks of incense smoking from a vase of marigolds on a wooden shelf, along with a plate of cookies and a gourd penis sheath decorated with bright red tadpoles—or are they lizard prints?

I wait in the waiting room. One hour while the plane refuels and the toilets are pumped. One hour in a shabby airport on the shimmering planet—footholds gone, chance-patterns in operation—between continents and time zones. As I take a seat and begin to ponder my surroundings, a grass-skirt band from Irian Jaya's logging-scarred interior ambles in and begins to shake out melodies on tiny guitars. To its accompaniment, barefoot adolescent girls stamp the floor, circle and shuffle in a dark wave-crest of beat. As they move, they form the shape of Pacific atolls. They are young and their music is for tourists, but their faces, perceived closely, reveal the lineage of a wise and ancient race recreating its ancient migration routes. The dance is a petroglyph in motion, a fluid symbol outlined with the feet—a design completely intact before humans even existed but nevertheless remembered by these dancers. Or, no, not "remembered" but simply brought to life from the unconscious, made visible by the language of movement.

Now a white-whiskered leather-skinned man joins the three butt-bumping girls and the two guitarists. He lowers his beat-up bass fiddle flat against the floor, rests one knee on its wooden body and begins to plucks its strings. To his booming syncopation tropical birds flitter in and out of the airport corridor. Then a Bo-Diddly-like voice crackles fuzzily through an overhead speaker and announces "Reboard." Quickly, the tourists—so engrossed a moment ago—hurry out the door onto the runway like schoolchildren having heard the end-of-recess bell. A few toss coins into a straw hat. Not payment enough, I am afraid, for the spirited output of these ragged, displaced musicians.

※

Built into the seat in front of me is a calling-card phone. Strange concept, to be aloft in the strobe of planetary flotsam, wondering who I might call (if I had a credit card). I think of my deceased mother whose atoms must surely circle this globe; my father—almost 90—living in the humidity of the same Michigan river town where he was born. I think of my ex lover now living with her own ex lover in Santa Barbara; my crazy composer friend pilgrimaging through New Zealand; the mysterious girl who gave me a necklace of jasmine on the beach at Mahabalipuram. I fantasize calling Joan of Arc, William Blake, St. Francis, Han Shan, Nikos Kazantzakis, Frida Kahlo, Marilyn Monroe or my hero of teenage years—John Muir.

As I ponder the magic of telecommunications (and the implied limitations), the plane free falls. There is a series of bumps, menacing monsoon clouds are piled high, the whole fuselage begins to creak. With a bit of panic I reach out to grab the armrests—noticing that the Chinese businessman across the aisle from me puts down his stocks-and-bonds report and calmly does the opposite: reaches *in* towards his solar plexus and cups his palms one over the other, as if to gather and contain energy rather than give over to fear.

An attractive Japanese woman, though, is not so calm. She begins to whimper, and with each bump her whimper reaches a higher pitch. The increasing intensity of her meow-like screams fills the fuselage with a kind of sexual ecstasy. Her husband, looking rather nonplused, offers her his arm. But she continues to scream the communal terror we all feel but won't allow ourselves to vocalize, and in that respect she plays a strange but necessary role for the rest of us. At the same time, there is something so vividly erotic about her escalating whimpers that it brings an embarrassed smile to each passenger's face. We've heard that climaxing sound only in private moments and now here it is, made public, as we all bump and roll together on a bed of purple thunderheads 30,000 feet above the planet.

⚹

Over the Indonesian archipelago we at last regain steady course. Below is the island of Flores with its sawed-off peak, Kelimutu, the famous volcano whose crater holds three supernatural lakes: one aquamarine, one sanguine, one sky blue. The Chinese gentleman shows me a 5000 Rupiah Indonesian bill, extravagantly printed with an exact full-color etching of the lakes. He tells me that all three bodies of water are joined below the surface. Influenced by the mineral content of Kelimutu and the energy charge of their separate fluids, their waters constantly change color. For me they symbolize the Father-Son-Holy Spirit trinity of my Catholic upbringing; the Shiva-Brahma-Vishnu triad of Hinduism; the Wisdom-Insight-Compassion trilogy of Buddhist thought. Finally, they remind me of the high mountain tarns of the Sierra Nevada. The ever-changing icy green and indigo pools at the base of sheer granite cliffs in Yosemite and Sequoia—landscapes that inspired me as a youth.

When I was ten, my father walked me through a lush green meadow bisected by a gurgling brook. Sun rays spread through giant redwoods, one of which had long ago fallen. It had been lightning struck and hollowed by fire. In the late 1800s a sheepherder repeatedly used the tree as a summer home, boarding up the fire-hollowed end except for a small window and midget doorway. In the cathedral light of the towering forest, invigorated by the smells of redwood and wildflowers, I stared through the door into the hermit's cabin. There was a fire pit with a tripod. A plankboard bed. A rustic table with a log stool. It was the first time I had witnessed the possibility of such a lifestyle. That hermits actually existed. That life could be lived simply, within the bounty and solitude of nature. I smelled the musty darkness of the tree's interior, felt the warm high-mountain sunlight on my body—and experienced a lifting sensation, as if my toes were floating above the softly-needled path. Most of all, I felt an incredible, tingling silence.

I suppose if I could use the "convenience" phone in the rear of the seat in front of me, I'd give a long-distance call and wake the spirit of dear old John Muir. I'd ask him about snow banners and wolverines and hidden trails still unfound by Sierra hikers. I'd describe for him these tropical clouds, fat as pomegranates atop Ionic columns, juicy and swollen with ionization that flavors the mouth with electricity. I'd remind him that the world has gotten very fast and very fat since his time, with far too much information and not enough understanding; that we are losing access to ecstasy, and that the imagination has been on the endangered-species list for some time now.

※

Three hours after leaving Biak, the plane lowers over Pulau Serangan (Turtle Island) in approach to a narrow spit of swampy land between mainland Bali and the peninsula of Bukit Badung. A feeling of landing right in the sea, and indeed I am ready for the plunge. The air becomes stifling as we lower. Moisture invades the fuselage, flight attendants hurry to collect glasses and headphones, their silhouettes caught in streamers of equatorial sun. Words slip from my journal, a stray hair coils into a spiral on the blank page.

Once again, the sensation of not knowing exactly where I'm bound. Even more to the point, I've lost track—through the long and displacing night—of where I've come from. Now that day has arrived I no longer see my reflection in the porthole, only the full brilliance of the world, the bigness of it, the seemingly aimless circus-colored scooters and taxis ant-like along blacktop arteries, banana-loaded Toyotas puffing black punctuations of diesel exhaust, an open-air market with dot-and-dash stick-figure shoppers ambling and haggling, a few roofless temples abandoned to dry patches of cactus and broken stone walls, plenty of ugly highrise hotels with their chlorinated swimming pools, bathers topless on a kiosked beach, and towards Bali's interior: morning fogs, hazy lime-green terraces and darkened thunderheads mounting the sensual roll of volcanic uplift.

Soon I'll be bathed by heat and monsoon, gestured toward the eruptive center of the garden, lowered into a green ravine, blown forth from the embered core of the volcano—a deviant of myself, imagining, experiencing, recreating the world through the altered perspective of travel.

※

THE KECAK DANCE AT PELIATAN

They eat dragonflies here. They carry fruit on their heads and grow mole hairs and fingernails to extraordinary lengths. They expose their teeth and buckle their lips to replicate the exact chatter and hiss of a monkey tribe. Or puff their chests to exhale the *Bo Bo Bo Bo Bo Bo Bo Bo Bo Bo Bo* of a gamelan gong. Men dress human or animal, male or female, carve stone into flashing eyes, sculpt a hill into a archetypal labyrinths of running water. Women weave palm and banana-leaf offerings, embellish them with marigolds and hydrangeas, set them to the four directions, place them in tree crotches, along river banks, at the base of oiled lingams, on stereo speakers and dashboards.

Bali is its own scene. In every courtyard there's a miniature temple smoking with incense that replicates the big mountain to the east, Gunung Agung—its volcanic cone thrust into the cloud-studded sky, its cold waters running like Shiva's tangled dreadlocks through rainforests down into rice fields. From somewhere, between banana leaves and coffee trees, comes a waft of sound from a practicing gamelan. Girls moving their feet. Boys learning the Kecak—the monkey chant.

The Balinese belong to their music. They speak with their eyes, release language from their fingers like bees from a hive. Their religion is based largely on the old animism. It encircles their thought systems, weaves dream with waking state, enchants daily life with awe and astonishment. In every act—a morning greeting, the flick of the eyes between women carrying loads on their heads, a boy climbing chameleon-like toward the heights of a coconut palm, a girl bending to place a flower offering in the temple garden—there is recognition: earth as household of the gods, body

171

as dwelling place of the supreme. The self is a living temple, to be swept and kept clean, to be washed and fed properly. Nothing goes unnoticed. Everything has significance, rhythm, voltage, a gelatinous transparency.

Life in Bali is continuously rejuvenated through honor of beauty in the superior as well as in the commonplace. Words rise and collapse with fragrance, fire, magnetism. The island blinks—a floating eye in a translucent sea; a shimmering jewel calling the visitor into multi-faceted spectacles of dance, drama, song, music, parades, pageantry of cremation smoke and gongs, fruit offered to the heavens, flowers sprinkled on the shoulders and feet. "Breathe of life!" the island says. "Inhale the juice of it, the force of it, the succulent tendrils of it. Breathe of an upper intelligence, of a magnificence magnified. Breathe down deep. Breathe out a sexual, fertile gesture. Wake, rise to the morning star, wash to the song of insects, let the mists lotion the flesh, let the coffee settle in the glass. Exhale the shadows of night, watch the air inside you enter the world, become a screen of foliage, a troupe of shadow puppets, a green sun, a woman the color of a purple orchid." Paul Gauguin did not come to the tropics to paint anything he did not see.

Distinctly, I remember my arrival in Bali. I was not yet beyond the gates of the modest international airport when I heard music in the air. Most of the passengers had already departed in tour buses, taxis and shuttles. I lingered outside the main terminal watching quick puffs of clouds grow fat in a breezy sky, hearing the sounds of whistles and flutes. A customs man, in brown and gold uniform (straight out of a Rousseau canvas), pointed toward the tops of two swaying palms. Between them circled a flock of doves. Each bird had a bamboo wind whistle tied to its feet. Someone had carved those whistles, brought them to market and sold them to the owner of the doves who had a fancy for music.

Earlier, the customs man had asked me to fill in the occupation blank on my entry papers. I wrote "artist." He looked up at me with a broad smile. "Do you paint?" "—Yes." "Abstract or realist?" I was floored. In thirty years of travels, I'd never been met by a customs man who smiled and stamped my papers with open acknowledgement of my vocation. He went on to explain that he had three brothers—one a stone carver who also etched scenes from Ramayana stories on palm leaf; the other a schoolteacher who doubled as a musician for the women's legong performances; the third a dancer who carved masks. When I told him I was en route to Ubud, he saw me to cheap local transport a few hundred meters from the airport (the bemo stop), urged me to see the Kecak Dance at Peliatan village, then waved me off with a "*Selamat Jalan.*"

※

In retrospect I have only scattered notes about the Kecak Dance. "Dance" is only a loose, generic term derived from the west that hardly fits the multi-layered, exquisitely-varied ritual performance of Bali. There is a similarity back home. In New Mexican pueblos "dance" refers to ritual choreography. Most tourists don't know that when they arrive. They expect a staged performance built into a convenient hour's duration and are hardly prepared for the real thing: a highly sacred village rite commencing at dawn and, without break, lasting through the heat (or snow) of day until dusk. Masked and painted dancers move to the beat of a drummer and the chant of singers in the open air of an earthen plaza between a conglomerate of adobe dwellings whose flat roofs are stacked with kindling and deer antler. A dozen to several hundred dancers; a half-dozen to over a hundred singers. It all happens not by clock, but in accord with the prayers in the kiva, the movement of the heavens. And always with great flexibility. "Indian time," some call it. In Indonesia, *"jam berapa,"* rubber time.

In Bali, every village enjoys open-air theater. Street, soccer field, graveyard, temple, neighborhood courtyard: wherever there is open space, that is the stage. Bare earth or hand-woven matting for a floor; palm thatch or a starry sky fringed with overhanging trees for a ceiling. For tourists there are scheduled, shortened versions of these village performances where masked and costumed dancers move to the rhythm of a gamelan, their story lines spoken or chanted to the sound of gongs, bells, drums and xylophones. Wry dialogues of clowns keep things in balance—just like in Hopi sky villages or in New Mexican pueblos. Often, as in the Kecak performance, there is the chatter and antics of forest creatures. *"Tjak tjak tjak tjak!"* call out the monkey impersonators, who do not 'dance' at all but move back and forth, side to side—hundreds of them seated in a tightly-knit circle, their bodies flattening and rising to the chant, their arms waving, fingers extended—from which the sound, the very seeds of each chanted word, spark and fly.

Dance! A combustible energy, a grouping of human stars in mythic constellations, an explosion of psychic energy manifest in an intense "burn," an adventurous beat, a a rising fountain of gestures, echoes, resonances. Deceptive vocal acrobatics that flutter in and out the ribcage of the performer to lodge in the body of the observer, creating a stage without boundaries. Dance: *"to stretch out"*—from Old High German: *danson*—and in the stretching of one's limbs, to transform the body, make it larger than life, surpass the boundary of the flesh, assume another identity.

The Cak, or Kecak (often referred to as the Ramayana Monkey Chant), is a modern creation, rooted in the ancient Balinese sanghyang, or trance dance. I first heard a recording of a Kecak performance in Bali by ethnomusicologist David Lewiston in the late 1960s. The longplay album had these notes:

> "In a temple courtyard, more than 200 men squat in tight concentric circles around a small central space reserved for the chief protagonists. Suddenly, their sharp cries of *tjak* begin one of Bali's most thrilling musical experiences . . . Ostensibly, the *ketjak* is a reenactment of the battle described in the Ramayana epic—in which the monkey hordes came to the aid of Prince Rama in his battle with the evil King Ravana—complete with a chorus imitating monkeys, as they chant the syllable *tjak*."

Two decades later, in 1986, Lewiston again visited Bali, and though things had changed, the island had become crowded with tourists and many of the famed gamelan performers and composers had died, the old magic was still to be found. Once again he had the opportunity to witness the Kecak singers, supplementing his recording with these notes:

> "The *kecak* is uniquely Balinese. (It) came into existence in the 1930s, when the a famous Baris dancer named Limbak was encouraged by the German painter, musician, and ethnologist Walter Spies (who played an active role in the island's cultural life at that time) to adapt this traditional musical form within a new context—a performance of (a segment of) the classic Ramayana story."

One afternoon I wandered Ubud's monkey forest, a ravine filled with towering trees and dense vines, lush remains of once extensive tropical woodlands before they were cleared for fields and inns. Smart, tricky all-powerful monkeys were everywhere: meditating on boulders, sitting on the trail begging food from tourists, subtly protecting or aggressively claiming their forest with weird cries from high tree tops. Feared by foreigners, respected by the Balinese, they reminded me of the swift and witty participants of the mythic Ramayana battle led by the supermonkey, Hanuman—whose job it was to fly with his band of warrior monkeys to the magic isle where evil king Ravana held Prince Rama's wife Sita, and rescue her (the story operates on many levels, alluding to the restoration of male/female energy, the rejuvenation of psychic balance through the reunification of yin/yang principals).

Auspiciously, on my return from the monkey forest, I passed a man and wife sitting on a doorstep who invited me to share a glass of thick Balinese coffee and a couple of sweet cakes. During our conversation I learned that the man made about 5000 rupiah a day teaching high school—about $2.50 for a nine to one-thirty routine. His wife earned even less at a nearby pharmacy. 2000 rupiah of their sum pay went towards daily child care for their two young girls. But, what most fascinated me was that nightly the man turned into a monkey. From seven to nine he joined the Semara Madya group at Peliatan for Kecak rehearsals. When he pulled out a pad of little pink tickets for one of the performances, I didn't hesitate to buy one (the 2000 Rupiah purchase price was nearly half the man's daily wages as a teacher) and that evening found myself in Peliatan, waiting under the stars for things to begin.

The performance was held in a simulated temple courtyard, a large square cement pad swept with bunches of grass and—along with the Kecak performers—sprinkled with water by a Hindu priest. Compared to the eighty-plus Kecak members, the audience was small: less than a third of

176

that number, mostly foreign visitors. At length a large torch was lit at the center of the pad. Its many wicks at first looked like a burning spine. As the performance progressed I reglimpsed the torch many times and saw it as a symbolic tree, a human torso whose branches spread the primal flame of inner illumination into the darkness (ignorance) of the world.

Each performer was naked except for a wrapping of *kain poleng*—black and white checkered cloth—around his waist, and a red hibiscus behind one ear. The dancers entered the stage area from the tropical darkness, standing, their monkey-like silhouettes hunched and shaking, arms dangling puppet-like, the wide-open whites of their eyes glazed with an edge of suspense, the audience filled with anticipation. Then—with the sway of all heads in unison—a calling out of an eery chant. Pure voice, no gamelan. Spiraling downward with a fluttering of hands, they collapsed into a crosslegged sitting position, backs firm, eyes out of focus, wild half-grins across their mouths, a great crescendo of high-pitched voice rising from their collective gestures. An unearthly chattering filled the shadows! I was pulverized by sound, my mind liberated from all thoughts by a powerful energy radiating through the night—a spasming, upward-climbing vibratory architecture of rhythm spat and chattered through clenched mouths, repetitively rising to a scary turbulence, abruptly lowering to a hushed, almost choral singing.

When I looked again, it was impossible to single out any one member of the Kecak troupe. All of the participants had merged into one perspiring, writhing mass of tentacles, torch light wavering over their single sweat-prismed body. The thick air trembled with succulent oscillations released through that body, absorbed again by that body—through the receding coil of fingers into hands, hands into arms, arms into torso and, finally, all of the men's sweating torsos reclining on top of one other. At

177

that point the entire troupe took on the appearance of one of those monstrous Sumatran *rafflesia* flowers that, after opening and spreading its giant petals, now began to wither, drawing in its fleshy mass to a perspiring purplish center.

Flower of flesh! Anemone of burning sound! Womb flower breathing in and out with a hallucinatory vibration of *Bo Bo Bo Bos* and staccato *tjaK! tjakka tjakka tjakka tjaKs* all unified into an overpowering chant, now and then a single voice recognizable within it all, a kind of high-pitched wail giving counterpoint to the overall pattern of haunting melody—all these male bodies simultaneously multiplying with identical gestures and rhythm into a single sexual form: the female vulva from which every male is born.

The power of performance in Bali implies the ability to transform many bodies into a single body, and to transport the audience out of its body into a kaleidoscope of imagery—no tricks of electricity, studio play, dub, overdub or soundboard overlay. Just the interlocking acapella, a phrasing and rephrasing of sound by earth-naked symbolic bodies chanting and gesturing the perceiver into the Other World. As Antonin Artaud said: "developed to the nth power and definitively stylized."

Afterwards, walking under a misty moon splintering its rays through the lace of a huge banyan, I was confronted by a pack of nasty dogs edging in at me from the doorfronts along a narrow lane. Remembering the swaying Kecak singers—elbows held angularly out at shoulder level, seated bodies vibrating with puffs and whoozes of inhaled air, suddenly rising like a storm of crazed giants erupting with eery, crackling energy—I gathered oxygen in my lungs and made myself quickly tall, hissing, fluttering my arms like the Peliatan monkey men. Success! With a whining prance, the

178

mutts dispersed, cowering to the safety of cobbled porch steps and shadowed alcoves.

Smiling, I continued past oddly-tilting neighborhood temples, enjoying only the sound of my flipflops on cobble. With the still-reverberating chant of the Kecak performers in my body, one thought kept resounding: "Life here is borne from the stage—motion and emotion merged into a mysterious, quavering vocabulary of pitch and timbre, sinuous movement and symbolic gesture. The flesh steals away from itself in alchemical dance, becomes a gilded sound pattern—like the magical warp and weft of double-ikat designs given by Indra to the ancestral Balinese in their remote forest hideaways."

※

This morning, passing those same temples, I turn a modest glance towards a young dancer practicing in a pavilion. Wrapped in elegant cloths printed with anthropomorphical figures and flowers, she dips and quickens her sidestep. Gunung Agung, Bali's sacred mountain, rises into the sky behind her like a winged headdress, a cloud to either side of its lavender crest. With pendants of rain and sweat, splashed by the holy water of Hindu priests, the dancer's flesh exudes a tropical perfume—champa, frangipani, oil of sandat. Bound in textiles of violet stars and crimson phoenixes, she lifts and spins, darting spear-like glances as she climaxes to the music of the gamelan, sweat rolling down through her breasts to her trembling navel.

Here, humans change places with a hierarchy of gods and goddesses. Old stories truly survive and regenerate a continuous contemplation and examination of good and evil. Psychic forces manifest in societies called

179

"primitive" (*first*) are definitely manifest in 20th-century Bali—and in fact take precedence over the written word. Theater, everyday life, prayer, dance, death, childbirth, agriculture, art, religion, lovemaking and clowning in Bali are all and forever somersaulting.

Despite its commercial aspects, the island retains its image of a "lost paradise"—not of bare-breasted women and unimaginable creatures lurking under smoking volcanoes entwined with primeval plants—but of a race perpetually renewing itself, endowed with a sense of humor, balance, centeredness and style, living in true correspondence with nature on a superbly creative and refined level—always an exceptional concern for beauty, transformation, the occult and the divine.

In Balinese performance there is a blissful, almost maddening making visual of the unconscious realm, a recognition of and reckoning with the Other World. Sacred and secular, dark and light, water and fire, work and play, stage and street, house and temple, woman and flower, monkey and man, dancer's hand and worker's plow, human clock and celestial wing—all merge in a great stream. Rice sprouts by moonlight, drums resound, fireflies alight and dance, ants carry their loads under the flaming zodiac, indigo turns carnelian with song, the ephemeral is momentarily solid, the solid, fluid. A million chattering monkeys rattle the forest. Fish dart and fall silent in rippling pools as gong and gender soothe the night with a quavering andante.

Pliant limbs, slippery path. The art of body movement is to the Balinese as simple as breathing. The vitality of music extends from the stylized gestures on the flower-petalled stage to the whoosh of a metal smith's bellows, to the splash of a fisherman's net, to the noodle vendor's banging sticks or a mother's hand rocking a baby in a woven cradle. There is an almost choreographed daily movement from stone gate to green field, village mud to city asphalt, black sand to sea-foam translucence, a blubbering outboard motor, the voice of a puppet master, the throat-clearing washerwoman slapping her knotted sarongs on a river boulder. Tempo, measure, intricate patterns of walking, lifting, bending, sowing. The sift of wind through a catamaran sail, splash of salt-wave over a prow of painted eyes, clonk of the duck-herder's cane, call of the papaya vendor's lusty voice. Music is in the gamelan and in the muscles, flexing from arms and toes through every stage of life, the blood of birth to the flames of the pyre. To embark on the journey is to participate in the Mystery, have dialogue with the Occult, present offerings to the Unseen, keep house with the Divine.

Kecak is only one of hundreds of performances enjoyed throughout Bali on a daily basis. There is a uniqueness about its silent tension, the suspense preceding the quiet suck and loud exhalation of air from the performers' lungs. It is a dance rooted in exorcism. Every movement is one of purge and purification—each flap and chatter, the repeated mantra of hisses, the tangled half-spitting bodies massing and collapsing, swaying and roaring—as if to replicate an ocean's blow hole, or the eruptive force of a rumbling volcano, the sweat of lava running down its flanks under the stars and mists.

Joyous, manic, sometimes morose, constantly startling the senses—dance provides emotional equilibrium within the framework of the everyday. There is more continuous dance on Bali than anywhere else in the world. Music bursts, arrowy fingers join and part in sexual mudras. The dancer becomes a drunken egret. The gamelan replicates the splash of jewels dumped from an urn, a gush of rain from tin eaves, crickets chirping, bees humming, frogs rasping, monkeys in amorous play, insects iridescently stirring in forest leaves, coffee grinding, kites flapping, a baby suckling, a truck overloaded with custard apples downshifting into low, lovers kissing, bamboo creaking in the breeze.

Gonging reverberation, metallic ting, cooing drones. White-masked monkeys roar and glide through the sky as if given expression by Chagall. Firecrackers bang. A motorbike chatters obscenely through a starlit garden. Yards of gold silk are gathered around thighs and buttocks. Beards are pasted, tails pinned.

Purposeful silence, amazing gutturals. Stammering barks, clickclack tongues, wide-spread legs, pirouette twirls. The fingers purr, liquid hips rise in glittering circles. A drummer vigorously accentuates soft flights of in-and-out ecstasy. Perceiver does not exist apart from perceived. Senses exist not in head or heart but extend like cilia from every pore of the body, gathering images and impressions: dragonflys diaphanously lovemaking; newlyweds entwined in a crisscross of incantations, dreaming the undreamed.

It's all a labyrinth, a sacred maze where imaginal pictures join the originals from which they were born. A garden, an island, a cosmography where gods, humans, griffins, witches, chattering monkeys, the piquant troublemaker, the courtesan with fluttering fan all become lost, roll together, shadow box, give up their masks—and find balance.

※

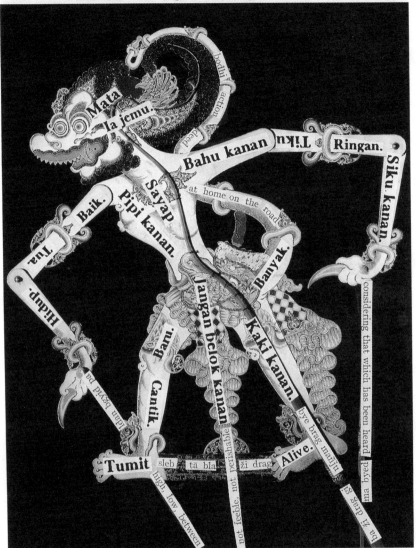

WAYANG KULIT: the Balinese Shadow Puppet Play
& the Magic Power of the Word

Monsoon in Bali. Watery green everywhere. Flowering vines and leafy tangles silhouetted against a mother-of-pearl dusk. A lone man, bare except for shorts and a triangular reed hat, walks a narrow, handbuilt levee in the center of a flooded rice field. His lean silhouette is lit by a bobbing lantern tied to a bamboo pole—along with a fresh catch of frogs. A near-full moon rises over row after row of intricately-spaced rice plantings. Directly into its luminous face the farmer walks, growing smaller and smaller, until he disappears where the paddies drop into a steaming ravine.

In this heightened season of rains, afternoon storms pound the hill town of Ubud with daily regularity, but nobody seems to mind. Moss grows greener by the second, crawling right up stop signs, brick walls and wooden shrines. Plumeria, orchids, sprays of bougainvillea and flaming poinsettia luxuriantly decorate every meticulously-tended Balinese courtyard. The island greets its inhabitants with wilder and wilder riots of flowers each morning. By midday, piling cumulus have darkened the landscape. Rains gush from enormous cloud pillars and splash right onto the pot-bellied deities crouched inside their weathered temples. Children wisely reel in their paper kites when the thunder bellows. Raindrops pizzz and pop from the heads of market shoppers, but umbrellas open and transactions playfully continue. A few men appear from pink and yellow doorways to fetch their fighting cocks from sidewalks where they've been caged under bell-shaped baskets. Duck herders and rice sowers seem to be the only ones with no mind for cover—save for the ubiquitous geckos who remain unblinking between electric-green branches, and the lovers beneath them who share a clove cigarette, staring heavenward in quiet ecstasy after a quick, midday nap.

Predictably, the drench lets up by dusk and the clouds part to reveal the Southern Cross. Ketut, the young owner of my homestay, informs me that tonight there will be a *wayang kulit* performance at the neighborhood temple. He fastens my batik sarong with a bright saffron-colored sash, ties a white cotton band around my head, and pushes me off toward the sound of a practicing *gamelan*. It's a few blocks away through a slippery cobble alley walled with lush growth, lychee trees drooping with ripening pods, hibiscus everywhere, and an occasional shrub loaded with intoxicating datura blossoms. On both sides of the path rise festive *penjors*: twenty-foot-high bamboo poles decorated with coils of palm frond and scrolled strips of banana leaves, bent with dangling fruit clusters and palm-leaf ornaments. The *pura*, or temple complex, is a walled collection of thatch-roof pavilions, courtyards and multi-storied pagodas with pointed grass roofs. There is a wooden tower with two hollowed-log bells suspended vertically from its ceiling. Through a ceremonial gate I can see various cloth-wrapped shrines loaded with fruit and smoking incense. Here, priests bend to bless kneeling families with holy water. The gate, known as the *candi bentar*, is unique to Balinese architecture—a sort of hewn-stone tower tapering rapidly toward zenith, yet with a seam of open sky right down the middle, as if split by lightning. Through this narrow cleft I pass into the temple grounds, pass from secular to sacred. It's an impressive threshold, one that seems to symbolize the Balinese concept of *Sekala* (the visible; the stone) and *Niskala* (the occult; the cleft).

The shadow puppet troupe (*dalang*, attendants and gamelan) sets up inside a curtained kiosk, open at back, screened with unprinted muslin pulled taut in front. The kiosk is slightly apart from the temple, situated

186

in an open pavilion facing a narrow street—one of many radiating uphill from Ubud into the *sawahs*, rice terraces, and eventually disappearing into the tangled slopes of Bali's volcanic backbone.

I take a seat on part of the temple-complex steps, about twenty feet from the shadow-puppet screen. The screen is backlit by a kerosene lamp inside the kiosk. Gradually an audience gathers. Several dozen people, nearly all Balinese, smoke *kretek* cigarettes and munch satay and sweets purchased from lantern-lit stalls colorfully arranged at the temple entrance. Odors of spices are strong. Peanut sauces, curry, shredded coconut, cloves, coffee, black rice pudding sweetened with palm sugar. Even an occasional waft of *brem*—hearty locally-brewed rice wine.

A short distance off, a group of boys throw dice onto a square of oilcloth printed with crab, eel, garuda, carp and a coiled serpent—merrily gambling at the temple entrance. Above the boys is a shrine with a little thatched-roof open-air pavilion filled with coconuts, bananas, lychee, apples, gayly-colored sweets and smoking joss sticks—all piled in baskets on a stone platform wrapped with checkered "shrine cloth." It's the same black-and-white wrapping I've seen all over Bali, swaddling banyan trees and stone temple guardians or decorating important thresholds. I am told that the cloth—*kain poleng*—is a kind of Balinese symbol for yin-yang, a reminder of the interlocked drama of good and evil, and "the need to be at the center of each moment with awareness and balance."

At about 9:30, Orion exactly at zenith, the shadow puppet performance begins. And well into dawn it lasts.

I am wholly fascinated by the man behind the curtain: the dalang. For he is more than just the puppeteer. He is the central figure of the drama:

master performer, puppet maker, storyteller, joker, moralist, choreographer, operatic clown, priest, punmaker, psychic, musician, conductor, magician, charismatic showman, oracle, historian, improvisational trickster, singer, chanter, speaker of ancient *Kaw*, and of High, Middle and Low Balinese—not just dialects with slight differences, but completely separate tongues.

Wedged between smiling Balinese families and a few loners wrapped in rectangles of printed cotton and batik sarongs, I shift and relax into my own little nest, light a kretek cigarette, inhale the sweet pungence of tobacco and cloves—more out of social ritual than personal custom—and watch the wayang kulit unfold. I understand nothing of the language, but do I need to? The action is fully engaging, the comic relief obvious, the battles entertaining, the horseplay not unlike the summer plaza dances at Hopi—where I don't understand the language either, but feel perfectly at home with the characters. The intent of the drama is made clear largely by mime, gesture, warp and elongation of words, eery and exaggerated vocal intonations.

The cries and utterances of the dalang are often reduced to astonishing sound vibrations. I hear them not with my ears but with the entire body. Distortions and magnifications resonate within my muscular chambers. In the flickering shadowy darkness, language has become a medium, an entity with its own pulse and shape transporting the audience into altered consciousness. The moment words are uttered they enlarge, hover, dance and disintegrate with an evocative, mythic presence loaded with ambiguity and metaphor.

In this context, words have a personal presence. They are disconnected from meaning, but connected with gender, connected with the ability to create and destroy. They cannot be reduced to logic or utilitarian purpose. They can be received only through the doors of feeling, intuition, surrender. Tonight, under lunar-lit cloud draperies, the word is a magic vessel, revitalizing the mind, calling up its dormant energies.

Entertainment, yes, but with the power of creative sound that recalls the mantric tradition of India or Tibet where "words" are sonorous presences transcending definition. Pure, resonating creative force! Sound equivilants of experience. Not gibberish, but alchemical entities that give the body pictures, cause the mind to imagine.

The "midwife" of these words is the dalang—who is simultaneously a religious figure, entrusted to entertain not only humans, but the gods themselves. Midwife, because he nurses wet and fiery syllables from a pregnant state of darkness, cutting their cords one after another the moment they are born from the belly of the Unseen into the flames of the lamplit screen.

Antonin Artaud, mesmerized by the fusion of word and drama in Balinese theater, wrote: "This mannerism ... this excessively hieratic style ... with its rolling alphabet ... syncopated modulations formed at the back of the throat ... sonorous interlacing of musical phrases that break off short ... no transition from gesture to cry or sound ... compose a sort of animated material murmur in the air, visual as well as audible ... all the senses interpenetrate, as if through strange channels hollowed out in the mind itself ... a state prior to language."

Most Balinese don't understand Kawi—a literary language rooted in Sanskrit, developed in South India and carried to Java. They simply "know the story" by the silhouettes of shadow puppets propped against

189

the screen waiting to go into action, their good-guy or bad-guy features projected on the cloth. Good characters have refined, delicately pointed, almost feminine features, and are arranged to the right of the dalang. The bad—bulbous, fat and fanged—are to the left.

In the shadow play—as well as in Balinese thought—neither good nor bad is hierarchical. One doesn't conquer the other. In the psyche, and certainly on the shadow-puppet screen, both sides are honored. We see ourselves in the drama, bumbling, occasionally wise, sometimes valiant but more often caught up in buffoonery. We are shadows of the gods who also lose at gambling, mistake reflections for reality and falter along their paths of heroic deeds. The stories of the wayang kulit remind us that our human task is to move through each day and every drama with harmony, humor and flexibility. A certain give and take is needed to keep the self in balance on the highwire between dark and light, brilliance and madness.

When the dalang projects the shadow of a thin, hand-held pagoda-like *kayon* on the cloth screen, the signal is given. The play is about to begin. The kayon disappears until it is needed to indicate a scene change. Or, with the expertise of the dalang, it might become a cloud, the wind, sacred Mt. Meru (the world's central axis in Hindu cosmology), the mystical Tree of Life, or even an obstacle representing spiritual confrontation. Delicately cut from buffalo hide, the kayon reminds me of an upside-down heart on a stick, or a leaf from the giant banyan that Buddha sat under to gain enlightenment.

After an hour I am brave enough to follow a few spectators who move out from in front of the screen to stand or sit behind it for awhile. This is a great view, and totally permissible in Balinese shadow-play etiquette.

(When did you last get up from your seat in the middle of an off-Broadway play and duck behind the scene for an intimate glimpse of actors, props and musicians!)

Inside the kiosk I can watch the dalang, crosslegged in front of the oil lamp (hung by a chain from a bamboo crosspole), madly working his characters. Each puppet (*wayang*) is fashioned from the skin (*kulit*) of a water buffalo, delicately filigreed, elaborately highlighted with vermillion and gold, arms and legs made articulate with thin sticks. Glittering in the flame light, the leather puppets dart rapidly back and forth under the direction of the dalang's hands. On the other side of the screen, the audience sees only mysterious, shadowy shapes. Seated under the stars, one's imagination personalizes each character. Thus, as one Balinese told me, "we are free to hear the teaching, no distraction of color."

Behind the screen, though, one is perpetually distracted. Enjoyably so! The dalang moves his characters in a battle scene with lightning pace. The toes of his left foot clutch a wooden striker with which he punctuates the battle by *bangbangbangbangbanging* the puppet box next to him. A fine resonator! His voice groans convulsively, twists and falls unintelligibly in and out of the gamelan music played by four crosslegged musicians behind him, hammering away at their xylophone-like instruments—keyboards suspended over bamboo resonators in highly-ornate frames. Marvelously, they keep pace to every action of the dalang's faster-than-eye hand, every rise and drop of his tremulous voice. He chatters, sweats, swims with words, swings his arms like propellers, slamming the painted heroines and villains against the screen. To either side of him, a vast array of ornate shadow puppets waiting for action are stuck by their thin sticks into banana trunks. Two attendants (*ketengkongs*) feed the puppets to the master as the scene demands. One

191

of these attendants also refuels the oil lamp when it dims.

Around the musicians are men and boys, resting against the sides of the
kiosk, their bare feet and legs crossed one over the other, their sarongs,
flowery high-collared shirts and ornate headbands all of handmade batik.
No buttons, loops, stitches, belts, pockets, straps, cuffs, tucks, rolls or
zippers. To see them, ah, what a beautiful flood of color! The body is
dressed as are temples and food. Honored with transparent wraps, made
seductive, embellished with the designs of flora, fauna, ocean, peaks and
clouds. Nature is divine and the Balinese are divine in it. Fruit is wrapped
in colorful, symbolic textiles and offered to the gods before it is eaten.
Bodies too are wrapped in textiles for rites of death, marriage, tooth
filing, hair cutting, and for purification, exorcism and magical protection
ceremonies. Whether wrapped around tree trunks or the trunks of human
bodies, textiles are used to create an aura around these phenomena as well
as to give significance to and express reverence for the interconnectedness
of all things within the cosmos.

Seated at the foot of the screen, the dalang is without shirt. He sweats
profusely. His ornate burnt-sienna-and-indigo batik sarong is tucked into
his crotch to allow maximum foot and arm action. I am repeatedly
stunned by the powerful projections of his voice! As with the Hopi
kachinas dancing in the summer plazas of their Arizona sky villages,
there is a ventriloquist effect. Vibration of vocal chords is diffused into a
halo of sound. It fills the air as if spoken by an invisible higher power.
Sometimes the dalang bows and growls into his armpit, or lifts head to
ricochet his voice off surrounding bamboo screens. In that tremolo of
reverberating energy the word is made omnipresent. It is empowered with
mystery, magic and Knowledge. And the common Bread of it, the passing
and receiving of it, is true Communion.

Wayang kulit! It is always a two-way show. Behind the screen, omnipresent technicolor. Outside the screen, a haiku in black and white. Good and evil coexist, one ups the other, things fall out of balance. The master eventually reinstates harmony. Audience drifts in and out of Kawi, sleeps, wakes to clowning and risque jabs, livens to bawdy seductions, travels with heroes into the supernatural. Music shimmers. Roosters crow. The infamous Balinese dogs finally quit barking and curl up to snore. Sky lightens; Southern Cross fades. Pivoting constellations have been my ceiling most of the night. Plenty of magic alive in Indonesia—despite heavy invasion of diesel fuel and videos. The government puts its iron grips on national t.v. and takes the censer splicer to films and documentaries; but political commentary survives in hand puppet performances.

"Wayang kulit is advice in the form of entertainment," a 66 year-old Balinese shopkeeper tells me. "But electronics *are* intruding. Shadow plays are becoming less important than before. I love it, but the young are not so interested."

Back at Ketut's homestay there's a small courtyard with a weathered pavilion once reserved for storytellers. It now flickers with a new t.v.—purchased with profits made from tourists, like me, who rent his backyard bungalows. Nightly, the gnarled trees, bromeliads, weird clusters of epiphyllum and miniature thatch-roof temples surrounding Ketut's patio are lit by eery blue-white flashes of sitcoms and game shows. Quietly I join the family (ages 8-80) for an hour in front of a glitzy disco program, live from Jakarta. The worst of Javanese mini stars doing Elton John and a heavily-censored Madonna. Secretly, I remind myself that the most ancient form of television is wayang kulit. Create the world, bring creatures into it, add light and there becomes shadow. Tame fire inside a stone circle, stare into it and stories are born. Act out the stories in front of the flame and your shadow is transformed. A mysterious character larger than life is given "color" by the viewer's imagination. There are as many characters within one shadow as there are viewers.

India is the cradle of Indonesia's shadow play. The dalang knows hundreds of stories from the Ramayana and Mahabharata epics. He possesses amazing memory, and performs live—no microphones or amplifiers—for hours without break. The wild battles, buffoonery of clowns, heroic exploits of gods and goddesses, seductive mingling of lovers, seething puns of the underdogs—all are moved into action by the magic power of the word. In ancient times the traveling bards of India kept these stories alive. They still do today. As do the anonymous masters on the streets of Indonesia—through wayang kulit (puppet plays) or wayang orang (human plays).

The stage knows no boundaries. Humans play musical chairs with the gods. Good and evil are in continuous examination, constant interplay. Psychic forces obvious to the eye before written words took precedence are still obvious in Bali. Theatre, everyday life, prayer, dance, visions of the absurd, the magic in the mundane, the high ecstasy of trance: all mix with hallucinatory overlap. To be here is to live in the very heart of reality, the very heart of illusion.

Books sited:

The Devotional Poems of Mirabai / A. J. Alston
The Theater and its Double / Antonin Artaud
Taking the Path of Zen / Robert Aitken
The Power of Myth/ Joseph Campbell
The Secret Oral Teachings in Tibetan Budhist Sects / A. David-Neel
A Coney Island of the Mind / Lawrence Ferlinghetti
Annapurna / Maurice Herzog
A Blue Fire / James Hillman
Sanskrit Poetry / Daniel H.H. Ingalls, tr.
Selected Poems / Robinson Jeffers
The Saviors of God & *Journeying*/ Nikos Kazantzakis
Theory and Function of the Duende/ Federico Garcia Lorca
The Ramayana / R. K. Narayan
Zen Poetry / Lucien Stryk
Glimpses of Bengal / Rabindranath Tagore

Selected Books by John Brandi:

Heartbeat Geography: Selected & Uncollected Poems
Weeding the Cosmos: Selected Haiku
In the Desert We do not Count the Days
Shadow Play: Poems, 1987-1991
Hymn for a Night Feast: Poems, 1979-1986
That Back Road In Poems, 1972-1979
Diary of a Journey to the Middle of the World
Desde Alla